Christopher L. Schilling
The Therapized Antisemite

De Gruyter
Disruptions

Volume 3

Christopher L. Schilling

The Therapized Antisemite

The Myth of Psychology and the Evasion of Responsibility

DE GRUYTER

ISBN (Paperback) 978-3-11-134928-2
ISBN (Hardcover) 978-3-11-135352-4
e-ISBN (PDF) 978-3-11-134957-2
e-ISBN (EPUB) 978-3-11-134970-1
ISSN 2748-9086

Library of Congress Control Number: 2023948468

Bibliographic information published by the Deutsche Nationalbibliothek
The Deutsche Nationalbibliothek lists this publication in the Deutsche Nationalbibliografie; detailed bibliographic data are available on the internet at http://dnb.dnb.de.

© 2024 Walter de Gruyter GmbH, Berlin/Boston
Typesetting: Integra Software Services Pvt. Ltd.
Printing and binding: CPI books GmbH, Leck

www.degruyter.com

In memory of the victims of the Kibbutz Kfar Aza pogrom (October 7, 2023).

And in honor of the heroes of Kibbutz Nir Am (October 7, 2023).

if often he was wrong and at times absurd,
to us he is no more a person
now but a whole climate of opinion
W. H. Auden, "In Memory of Sigmund Freud"

The most mentally deranged people are certainly
those who see in others indications of insanity they
do not notice in themselves.
Leo Tolstoy, "The Devil"

Foreword

On the Modern Inability to Face the Reality of Evil

This book went into print shortly after the horrific Hamas attack on Israel on October 7, 2023, and at a moment an antisemitic surge of historical proportions unfolded across the world. Consequently, the book does not deal directly with the attack and the euphoric cheering it received by many across the globe (nor the apparent indifference by most people to the systematic torture and murder of Jews solely for being Jewish which reached a scale not seen since the Holocaust).

However, those pogroms sadly make *The Therapized Antisemite* even more relevant. Right after the rape, torture, slaughter, and kidnapping of innocent Jews – including peace activists, children, and Holocaust survivors – had occurred, and before Israel began to retaliate, some people attempted to justify the attack by attributing the terrorists trauma. After all, "hurt people hurt people". Or to speculate about their temporal insanity due to drugs.

Or, to ascribe the various defenders in the West mental health issues. Why else would they celebrate reports of rape and the beheadings of children on college campuses as "liberation" and "exhilarating". Why else would they not see the obvious fact that Hamas is a terrorist organization, and that their rule is oppressing the people of Gaza (especially gays and women) in horrific ways. The Western defenders acting against their own values must be experiencing some kind of temporal insanity, perhaps a psychological group phenomenon before ethics class, unmedicated anxiety disorders, or a lack of self-esteem. Or by resorting to other senseless explanations that psychologists often reflexively come up with whenever they encounter evil.

Yet, the terrorists who committed these unspeakable crimes (including their attempt to kill the peace process in the Middle East) are fully responsible, as humans and as members of Hamas. And so too are the people who diabolically celebrated the unfolding genocide on the streets from Sydney to London, and across social media to former elite universities across America, fully responsible for their actions. Those antisemites shall not be therapized by us but judged. Not explained by pseudoscience but confronted with the law and morality. And most harshly so.

Acknowledgements

I am most thankful for an encounter I have had with the UK-based Campaign Against Antisemitism back in 2016. What they showed me was how a volunteer-led charity can successfully dedicate itself to exposing and countering antisemitism through education and zero-tolerance enforcement of the law. I'm grateful to Gideon Falter and the entire team, but especially to Benjamin Gray for his unexpected and selfless support. He is a brilliant mind, and a most talented and courageous barrister, but most importantly a real *mensch*. Their dedication, hard work, and immense compassion to the victims of antisemitism became an inspiration to everything that followed, including to write this book. Yet, the ideas of this book are entirely mine alone. I'm grateful to the late Robert Jervis for having invited me as visiting scholar to Columbia University right after I finished my PhD in political science more than a decade ago, and at a time when Columbia was quite a different place to what one has to witness there these days. I am shocked and horrified by the unacceptable level of antisemitism in the fall of 2023, as well as the celebration of rape, torture, and genocide on campus. The moral and academic decay by many Columbia students, faculty members, and administrators alike make me grateful to have experienced Columbia before the abyss it gazed into started to gaze back. And Robert Jervis' work on political psychology has been most interesting to view from up close. I thank Lesley Klaff who cares and encourages, and Bernard Harrison for reading and commenting on an earlier version of chapter 1. Many thanks as well to the peer reviewers of the book for their valuable comments and suggestions, especially to the constructive comments and insights of Zbyněk Tarant. Naturally, any omissions are mine. Immense thanks are also due to the folks at De Gruyter, especially Julia Brauch for her fantastic editing, Barbara Gizzi for the cover design, and Anne Rudolph for being such a marvelous production editor. I am also grateful to Daniel Allenstein who took the time to read and comment on the manuscript. He is kind, supportive, and as insightful as a reader as he is as a friend.

Contents

Foreword —— IX

Acknowledgements —— XI

Introduction —— 1

A Definition of Antisemitism —— 8

Chapter I
Social Psychology —— 11

Chapter II
Clinical Psychology —— 29
    Psychotherapy —— 30
    A Problematic History —— 34
    Ideas About Antisemitism —— 41
    Pharma —— 48

Chapter III
The Way the World Goes Mad, and a "WEIRD" Understanding of it —— 52
    Creating Mental Health Issues —— 52
    An Americanization of Mental Health —— 57
    "WEIRD" People —— 59

Chapter IV
Psychohistory —— 63

Chapter V
Forensic Psychology —— 70
    Criminal Profiling —— 70
    Court Testimony —— 71

Chapter VI
Psychology and Policymaking —— 81

Conclusion —— 88

Bibliography —— 91

Introduction

Sarah Halimi was an Orthodox Jew in her sixties, a former kindergarten director, and alone at home, when on an April night of 2017 a man entered her apartment in the Belleville district of Paris and tortured her for half an hour as he chanted verses from the Koran and shouted "*Allahu Akbar*" and antisemitic slurs, while she cried for help. Her neighbours heard her cries, called the police, and gave the officers keys to her apartment when they arrived on the scene. "It is an older woman, and she seems to suffer a lot," one caller told the police.[1] Yet they refused to act until backup arrived,[2] later claimed not to have heard the death cries that had woken up the entire building,[3] and remained on the street when Sarah Halimi's tortured, but still living body fell to the pavement as the killer threw her out of the window of her third-story apartment.

However, citing Article 122 of the French Penal Code, judges declared the murderer not criminally responsible based on an independent psychiatric analysis. The reason: It was found that he was undergoing a "psychotic episode" due to cannabis consumption. The murderer's "discernment" had been "abolished."[4] Yet the court concluded that the killer's motivation to murder Sarah Halimi was the fact that she was Jewish.[5] The perpetrator had testified before the judge that he had not been in control of his senses, because a Jewish prayer book and a menorah in the victim's apartment had aggravated his mental state, and thus accusing her of having provoked him with Jewish ritual objects in her own home.[6] Regardless, the court ruled that the murderer should not stand trial but remain in a secure hospital, and that he "may be released from the psychiatric facility where he is held pending a recommendation by his doctors, if approved by a police com-

---

1 https://aish.com/sarah-halimis-murder-masking-jew-hatred-in-france/. Accessed August 23, 2023.
2 https://www.tabletmag.com/sections/news/articles/terror-anti-semitism-france. Accessed August 23, 2023.
3 https://www.timesofisrael.com/french-parliamentary-report-on-sarah-halimi-murder-reopens-wounds-it-sought-to-heal/. Accessed August 23, 2023; https://www.theguardian.com/world/2018/nov/27/how-the-murders-of-two-elderly-jewish-women-shook-france-antisemitism-mireille-knoll-sarah-halimi. Accessed August 23, 2023.
4 https://www.bbc.com/news/world-europe-56929040. Accessed August 23, 2023.
5 https://www.timesofisrael.com/french-parliamentary-report-on-sarah-halimi-murder-reopens-wounds-it-sought-to-heal/. Accessed August 23, 2023.
6 https://jewishchronicle.timesofisrael.com/french-parliamentary-report-on-halimi-murder-case-reopens-wound-it-sought-to-heal/. Accessed August 23, 2023; https://www.israelhayom.com/2021/12/23/sarah-halimi-affair-made-me-realize-frances-justice-system-is-dead/. Accessed August 23, 2023.

missioner."⁷ "The crime was the crime of a madman," wrote five of the psychiatric experts in the newspaper *Le Monde*, who thereby justified their opinions which had led to the horrific ruling, "And in France we do not judge the mad."⁸

The fact that the antisemitic murderer could successfully claim temporal psychosis⁹ has shockingly demonstrated that legal practise can lead to the most outrageous injustices when psychology is seen as *the* explanation of human behaviour, as if he had no choice but to kill her, as if life is one huge Stanford prison experiment.

In October 2020, during the Jewish holiday of Sukkot, a man took a taxi to the synagogue of the German city of Hamburg. Dressed in a camouflage suit and carrying a folding spade (as well as a swastika on a paper in one of his pockets), he got out of the taxi and went straight to a police officer and asked where he could find the synagogue. "Here in the security area," the police officer told him. "All right!," the man replied and, spotting a student wearing a kippah in front of the synagogue, proceeded to attack him with the folding spade and seriously injuring the Jewish victim.¹⁰ But, as a psychiatric evaluation found the attacker to suffer from paranoid schizophrenia, the public prosecutor did not see the case as an antisemitic act.¹¹ The German judge concluded in her judgement that the attacker's

---

7 https://www.timesofisrael.com/french-parliamentary-report-on-sarah-halimi-murder-reopens-wounds-it-sought-to-heal/. Accessed August 23, 2023.

8 https://www.lemonde.fr/idees/article/2021/04/25/affaire-sarah-halimi-le-crime-etait-celui-d-un-fou-ce-qui-ne-l-empeche-pas-d-etre-antisemite_6078022_3232.html. Accessed August 23, 2023. Thankfully, in December 2021, "the French senate passed a law nullifying temporary insanity defenses related to the voluntary ingestion of drugs," as reported by the Jewish Telegraphic Agency. See: https://www.jta.org/2022/01/21/global/french-parliamentary-report-on-the-sarah-halimi-murder-case-reopens-the-wound-it-sought-to-heal. Accessed August 23, 2023.

9 Cnaan Liphshiz, "French judge rules Jewish woman's killer not responsible because he smoked weed," *The Times of Israel* (16 July 2019).

10 https://www.welt.de/regionales/hamburg/article227168243/Angriff-auf-juedischen-Studenten-29-jaehriger-Taeter-muss-dauerhaft-in-die-Psychiatrie.html. Accessed August 23, 2023.

11 https://www.welt.de/regionales/hamburg/article227168243/Angriff-auf-juedischen-Studenten-29-jaehriger-Taeter-muss-dauerhaft-in-die-Psychiatrie.html. Accessed August 23, 2023; https://www.algemeiner.com/2021/02/19/german-jews-angry-at-prosecutors-decision-not-to-charge-hamburg-synagogue-attacker-because-of-mental-illness/. Accessed August 23, 2023; https://www.dw.com/en/german-court-commits-hamburg-synagogue-attacker-to-psychiatric-hospital/a-56719258. Accessed August 23, 2023; https://www.thejc.com/news/world/hamburg-trial-unnerves-jewish-community-1.511858?reloadTime=1651190400010; https://www.juedische-allgemeine.de/politik/ermittlungen-abgeschlossen-2/. Accessed August 23, 2023; Only in 2021 did the German parliament decide to include the term "antisemitic" in § 46 StGB *Grundsätze der Strafzumessung* (principles of sentencing). Nevertheless, public prosecutors in Germany had previously taken antisemitism into account as a possible aggravating factor in sentencing. But not in this case: https://www.bundestag.de/resource/blob/869658/483422dfea88196135fb07e92c2febbf/WD-7-101-21-pdf-data.pdf. Accessed August 23, 2023.

motivation was that the victim was "a member of the Jewish faith,"[12] but found him not criminally responsible because of a psychiatric evaluation,[13] as if a psychologist's opinion paper somehow negated the law, the quest for justice, and common sense, it seems. The attacker was not even ordered by the court to be present during his trial apart from its initial hearing, because it could have further deteriorated his mental health. A representative of Hamburg's Jewish community found words for the attack, and the terrible injustice that followed: "It must be recognized that we as a Jewish community are under threat. How are you supposed to prevent antisemitic acts in the future if you don't even call them antisemitic?"[14]

The answer is that we are decreasingly able to do so in a culture where psychology becomes *the* authority for assessing human behavior. What a "sick" man he must have been to be an antisemite, leaves not much space for personal responsibility and his actual antisemitic motive. After all, the sick man needs help. And so it has been argued in the case of the American poet Ezra Pound, who broadcasted antisemitic propaganda and praised Mussolini and Hitler over the radio in Italy during WW2. He avoided being tried for treason after the war as he was found incompetent to stand trial and put into a U.S. federal asylum. When the treason charges were dropped in 1958, he was released, returned to Italy, and spent the rest of his life in Venice.[15]

But how did we get to this level of injustice? At first there was a myth. A myth about a new scientific field that would enable us to understand the human mind, and to conquer feelings with thoughts, and thoughts with willpower. But for over a hundred years now, psychology's vision has remained no more than a myth in much of Western society. Despite its theories and concepts being widely criticized and often proven wrong, it remains a part of our culture, academia, and legal systems, and not just when it comes to judging antisemitic crimes. The idea that thoughts on their own can steer feelings, and that the new "science" of psychology reveals how to apply this technique the best way, was intriguing. The idea is that one is able to conquer sadness and despair simply by talking about it

---

12 https://www.welt.de/regionales/hamburg/article227168243/Angriff-auf-juedischen-Studenten-29-jaehriger-Taeter-muss-dauerhaft-in-die-Psychiatrie.html. Accessed August 23, 2023.
13 https://www.welt.de/regionales/hamburg/article227168243/Angriff-auf-juedischen-Studenten-29-jaehriger-Taeter-muss-dauerhaft-in-die-Psychiatrie.html. Accessed August 23, 2023.
14 https://www.welt.de/regionales/hamburg/article224013724/Angriff-auf-juedischen-Studenten-in-Hamburg-Ermittler-sehen-kein-politisches-Motiv.html. Accessed August 23, 2023.
15 A. David Moody, *Ezra Pound: Poet. A Portrait of the Man and His Work. III: The Tragic Years 1939–1972* (Oxford: Oxford University Press, 2015).

(or drugging it away), and that mentally healthy people treat themselves and others well, and accomplish things in life, and that the science of psychology offers a path to that benign human state, because it gives insight into how people think, feel, and behave, and how to change it. But it is a myth that nothing is good or bad, but that thoughts make it so, and that psychology can help one to restructure the mind by talking about our feelings. Salvation awaits those who rearrange their thoughts enough to be happy and at peace with all that is wrong in our times. Think yourself well! And if that does not work, drug your mind well!

However: "Is it really possible to tell someone else what one feels?,"[16] asks Tolstoy in *Anna Karenina*. Kafka wrote in a letter to his one-time muse Milena: "I can't explain to you or to anybody what it's like inside me. How could I begin to explain; I can't even explain it to myself."[17] If even the most talented writers struggle to express their inner lives, how could just any person do so through the interview methods of psychotherapy? It is a myth that a person can express one's inner life adequately in words. It is a myth that psychology creates better humans by re-arranging thoughts and feelings, or that it gives any insight into a person's level of agency. And even if we were able to express what we feel in just that moment in time, would it be meaningful? Hannah Arendt was on point in *The Life of the Mind* when she wrote that "psychology, depth psychology or psychoanalysis, can discover no more than the ever-changing moods, the ups and downs of our psychic life, and its results and discoveries are neither particularly appealing nor very meaningful in themselves."[18]

Nevertheless, the meaningless idea became the fabric of a field, and ultimately much of Western culture: We control our feelings with thoughts; think ourselves happy, slim, and wealthy; spend our time and money in therapy offices to heal from trauma by talking about it endlessly until one day it miraculously works; and ignore the impact of all other factors within the complexity of human life. If it works, it proves the truth behind psychology; if it does not, one needs only to apply oneself more thoroughly to the dogma. That was how it all started. Scientific psychology as a "climate of opinion"[19] was born. And it is in that climate our current justice system exists. The term "syndrome," for instance, was entirely absent in American law reviews in the 1950s, 60s and 70s, until in 1980 a single

---

16 Leo Tolstoy, *Anna Karenina* (New York: Penguin Classics 2004), 760.
17 Franz Kafka, *Letters to Milena*, (trans. Philip Boehm; New York: Schocken, 2015), 227.
18 Hannah Arendt, *The Life of the Mind: The Groundbreaking Investigation on How We Think* (New York: Harcourt, 1981), 35.
19 https://blogs.scientificamerican.com/literally-psyched/understanding-freuds-legacy-through-the-eyes-of-w-h-auden/. Accessed August 23, 2023.

article used the term, followed by a psychological explosion: 86 articles in 1985, 114 in 1988, and 146 in 1990.[20]

Ultimately, the tendency of psychology to explain all of human existence is harmful, because it suggests a solution to any human problem, even antisemitism. But, instead of hoping for the field of psychology one day to solve the problem of antisemitism, we must ask ourselves how much of this myth has not helped but rather harmed the fight against it. *The Therapized Antisemite* argues that we don't yet understand what causes antisemitism as a mental malfunction, let alone how to go about solving the problem, as psychology still fails to uncover the workings of the mind. Ultimately, we are confronted with a failure of an entire field, despite its prominent place in society, academia, and legal systems.

Academic studies of antisemitism are a subject with direct relevance for crime prevention and public policy. Yet, attempts to employ psychology in the field of antisemitism studies often lead to mixed, if not outright invalid or pseudo-scientific, results. Such studies can facilitate perpetrators of deliberate, violent antisemitic acts in escaping criminal prosecution and does not help to prevent its further spread. In exploring its social, clinical, and forensic applications, as well as the globalization of mental illnesses and psychohistory, *The Therapized Antisemite* seeks to change the way we think about antisemitism, psychology, and law.

I'm not denying that mental problems exist or arguing that they are simply a product of society. Mental malfunction obviously exists and matters,[21] but the view that the discipline of scientific (or rather academic) psychology helps to eliminate it, is a misconception, a myth. On the contrary, psychology is a dangerous endeavour, because it is an attempt to evade human responsibility for antisemitism. The term "responsibility" is, of course, ambiguous and a hotly debated topic in moral and legal philosophy.[22] "Responsible" is sometimes used as a synonym

---

[20] Donald Alexander Downs, *More Than Victims: Battered Women, the Syndrome Society, and the Law* (Chicago: The University of Chicago Press, 1996), 25.
[21] Robert S. Wistrich's *Antisemitism: The Longest Hatred* (New York: Pantheon, 1992), interestingly, does not reference to psychological literature while it speaks of terms such as "hysteria" and "fear".
[22] See for instance: H. L. A. Hart, *Punishment and Responsibility. Essays in the Philosophy of Law* (Oxford:Clarendon, 1968); Joel Feinberg, *Doing and Deserving* (Princeton: Princeton University Press, 1970); Alan R. White, *Grounds of Liability: An Introduction to the Philosophy of Law* (Oxford: Clarendon, 1985); John Martin Fischer and Mark Ravizza, eds., *Perspectives on Moral Responsibility* (Ithaca, NY: Cornell University Press, 1993); Jeannette Kenneth, *Agency and Responsibility* (Oxford: Clarendon, 2001); William Lucy, *Philosophy of Private Law* (Oxford: Oxford University Press, 2007); Walter Sinnott-Armstrong and Lynn Nadel, eds., *Conscious Will and Responsibility* (Oxford: Oxford University Press, 2011); Nicole A. Vincent, ed., *Neuroscience and Legal Responsibility* (Oxford: Oxford University Press, 2013); Walter Sinnott-Armstrong, ed., *Moral Psychology, Volume 4: Free Will and*

for "liable," "accountable," or "being the cause of." The form of responsibility that this book is concerned with is a combination of being legally accountable for antisemitic crimes and morally accountable for an antisemitic worldview.

Nor am I denying the value of the work some psychologists do with their clients. Their insights can be of value, as many of their recommendations may come from philosophy, literature, are lessons drawn from history or personal observation, rather than comprising psychological theorizing or the product of its experiments. But this book is not about the way psychology might assist victims of antisemitism. It is about the question of whether psychology can help us understand the phenomenon and its prevention and punishment. I am not a psychologist myself. This book presents the observations of a lawyer and political scientist who has been a visiting scholar at Columbia University[23] at the invitation of Robert Jervis, a pioneer in the study of the psychology of international politics. I have experience in training diplomats in understanding the role of emotions in foreign policy and have published on the topic of antisemitism and cognitive science.[24] Rather than structuring the book according to established streams and disciplines in psychology, it is thus divided by chapter according to various (and at times overlapping) fields of application. By being so structured this book forces the reader to think outside of established academic boxes. After all, isn't that what psychology is all about?

But in this context, one aspect must be clear right from the beginning: Some ill-guided attempts have been made by antisemites to claim that psychology is some kind of "Jewish science." And even some well-intended scholars make suggestions about psychology having been influenced by Freud's (or other early psychologist's) Jewish upbringing.[25] These suggestions are irrelevant. If psychology is a science, its findings are either right or wrong. Jewish this-or-that does not objec-

---

Moral Responsibility (Cambridge, MA: MIT Press, 2014); Jaap Hage and Antonia Waltermann, "Responsibility, Liability, and Retribution," in B. Brożek, J. Hage, and N. Vincent (eds.), *Law and Mind: A Survey of Law and the Cognitive Sciences* (Cambridge: Cambridge University Press, 2021), 255–288.

23 However, this was over a decade ago. These days I am perhaps not surprised, but nevertheless shocked and horrified by the unacceptable level of antisemitism and the mistreatment of Jewish students in the fall of 2023, as well as the celebration of rape, torture, and genocide on campus. The moral and academic decay by many Columbia students, faculty members, and administrators alike make me grateful to have experienced Columbia before the abyss it gazed into started to gaze back.

24 *The Japanese Talmud: Antisemitism in East Asia* (London: Hurst, 2023); "Why East Asia Matters to the Understanding of Antisemitism," *Journal of Contemporary Antisemitism* 6.2 (Fall Issue 2023).

25 See, for instance: Per Magnus Johansson and Elisabeth Punzi, "Jewishness and psychoanalysis – the relationship to identity, trauma and exile. An interview study," *Jewish Culture and History* 20.2 (2019): 140–152; DOI: 10.1080/1462169X.2019.1574429.

tively influence the falsity or truth determined by observation and experiment. To be clear: This book is an argument about psychology's part in the study and punishment of antisemitism, which is not to say that there is an automatic link between both fields, as if psychology were somehow Jewish. Yet some scholars describe psychology as a "Jewish science." When someone like clinical psychologist and professor at Birkbeck's Department of Psychosocial Studies, Stephen Frosh, calls the Jewish origins of psychology "a statement of what actually happened, and what has to be faced,"[26] the authority of a therapist seemingly blurs into academic psychology, where it does not belong. One does not "have to face" irrelevant facts in science. We only face those that matter, and that is what this book does.

---

26 Stephen Frosh, "Freud and Jewish Identity," *Theory and Psychology* 18.2 (2008): 167.

A Definition of Antisemitism

Before diving into the matter, a definition is due for clarity's sake. The term "antisemitic" is problematic for various reasons. It was first popularized by Wilhelm Marr, himself an antisemite. There are various definitions of "antisemitism," and even how the term should be written is disputed. I choose to write it as "antisemitism," as there is no "Semitism" for it to be against. As with many fields in academia, the definition of what constitutes as "antisemitic" itself is viciously debated. "Since at least 1879," writes Kenneth L. Marcus in *The Definition of Anti-Semitism*,

> the term "anti-Semitism" has been repeatedly, variously, and contradictorily defined and redefined in scores of lexicons, encyclopedia, and other reference works, as well as scholarly books and monographs. Despite these efforts, the question of definition is now more unsettled than at any previous time . . . because definitions are fraught with ideological assumptions that divide schools of thought.[27]

As the field of antisemitism research is shaped by these conflicts in which ideology and self-interest, research and the politicization of academia are often hard to distinguish, it constitutes an environment in which a clear definition of antisemitism does not appear easily. This leaves legal scholars with a dilemma.[28] We

---

27 Kenneth L. Marcus, *The Definition of Anti-Semitism* (Oxford: Oxford University Press, 2015), 6.
28 Giving the current rise in antisemitism, legal contributions to the question how to define the phenomenon seems all the more important. Yet, perplexingly, there is no institute for "Antisemitism and the Law" that could provide such a definition. I am not even aware of a law school offering a course on "antisemitism and the law" (while there are courses on Jewish religious law at law schools). Nor am I aware of a substantial body of research on antisemitism and the law. Examples are the "Law vs Antisemitism Project," a non-profit organization founded by two American law professors, Robert Katz and Diane Kemker. Fortunately, both seek to write a casebook on the topic with David Schraub (a project that by the time of this writing has not been completed), and organized the "Inaugural Law vs Antisemitism Conference" at Indiana University in 2022. (Yet, Derek Penslar, who is neither a legal scholar nor an expert on antisemitism and does not see the BDS movement as antisemitic, delivered the opening address. More about his scholarship in chapter IV. https://mckinneylaw.iu.edu/news/releases/2022/02/iu-mckinney-hosts-inaugural-law-vs-antisemitism-conference-.html (Access date October 26, 2023)). Among the few other scholars working on the intersection of antisemitism and the law are Reut Y. Paz and Thilo Marauhn with their "Seeing Antisemitism Through Law" project at the University of Giessen in Germany (https://www.uni-giessen.de/faculties/01/facultydep/liszt/satl) and their research partner Yoram Shachar of Reichman University in Israel (https://gepris.dfg.de/gepris/projekt/446952759). There is Robbie Sabel's work on international law and antisemitism at The Hebrew University of Jerusalem (Robbie Sabel, "A Role for International Law in Combating Antisemitism?" *Israel Journal of Foreign Affairs* 10.3 (2016): 451–456, DOI: 10.1080/23739770.2016.1247317), and David Seymour's work on the impact of the Holocaust on social and legal theory (David Seymour, *Law, Antisemitism and the Holocaust* (London: Routledge, 2007); https://londonantisemitism.com/about/).

need to judge antisemitism while we are not provided with a clear definition of what it is, but rather ongoing conflicts over its spelling, meaning, and research funding in an ideologically heated, and often inefficient and politicised academic climate. But what makes a crime "antisemitic" in a practical legal sense? The United Kingdom uses the definition of hate crime in general.[29] In 2021, 76 years after the Holocaust, the German parliament finally decided to include the term "antisemitic" into its principles of sentencing (§ 46 StGB *Grundsätze der Strafzumessung*). The US State Department follows the International Holocaust Remembrance Alliance (IHRA) "working definition,"[30] together with other members of the IHRA. So does the European Union.[31] The legal scholars Lesley Klaff and Derek Spitz have also argued in favour of adopting the IHRA definition by universities.[32] Hence, this book follows the common legal IHRA "working definition":

> Antisemitism is a certain perception of Jews, which may be expressed as hatred toward Jews. Rhetorical and physical manifestations of antisemitism are directed toward Jewish or non-Jewish individuals and/or their property, toward Jewish community institutions and religious facilities.[33]

Other scholars include the founder and chairman of the Louis D. Brandeis Center for Human Rights Under Law, Kenneth L. Marcus, as well as Steven H. Resnicoff (DePaul University College of Law), and Mark Goldfeder who serves as Director of the National Jewish Advocacy Center and as Special Counsel for International Affairs at the American Center for Law and Justice. He has written widely on the topics of law and antisemitism. See: https://brandeiscenter.com/about/board-of-directors/kenneth-l-marcus-esq/; https://brandeiscenter.com/about/academic-advisory-board/steven-h-resnicoff/; https://www.miryaminstitute.org/mark-goldfeder. And, of course, there is Lesley Klaff, who Kenneth L. Marcus correctly identifies as "one of the world's leading legal scholars" in the field of antisemitism studies. See: https://londonantisemitism.com/team/leslie-klaff-3/. Moreover, the research conducted by the UK-based Campaign against Antisemitism is noteworthy. Central to these works is the question of how to effectively use law to combat antisemitism. The contribution to this important and timely question offered by *The Therapized Antisemite* is to argue that part of the answer is to exclude psychology from the process. From theorizing about its origins to the courtroom, psychology does not help but harms the fight against antisemitism.

29 https://www.gov.uk/government/speeches/a-definition-of-antisemitism. Accessed August 23, 2023.
30 https://www.state.gov/defining-antisemitism/. Accessed August 23, 2023.
31 https://ec.europa.eu/info/policies/justice-and-fundamental-rights/combatting-discrimination/racism-and-xenophobia/combating-antisemitism/definition-antisemitism_en. Accessed August 23, 2023.
32 https://fathomjournal.org/why-the-2010-equality-act-does-not-make-the-ihra-definition-of-antisemitism-redundant/. Accessed August 23, 2023.
33 https://www.holocaustremembrance.com/sites/default/files/press_release_document_antisemitism.pdf. Accessed August 23, 2023.

This book is, however, not meant to add to ongoing debates over how to define the term, or how research positions are filled, or its spelling, but to make an important argument about the disturbing role that pseudo-science has come to play in the study and adjudication of antisemitism. For quite some time now, there have erupted such heated conflicts and attacks in the field that hardly any meaningful legal debate could have possibly taken place, lasting definitions been provided, and the obvious mistake been noticed that psychology has no justifiable place in any of it.

Chapter I
Social Psychology

With most of social psychology, as was once said about Freud, "what is new in these theories is not true, and what is true is not new."[34] Having been relatively speculative in its early beginning, social psychology is now meant to comprise the empirical investigation and scientific study of individual behavior in social and cultural settings. The field is shaped by different theories and conceptual schemes, with much of its impetus coming from American academics. Additionally other fields of psychology such as psychoanalysis, learning theory, and cognitive approaches, are conceptually influential. Its research often receives quite a lot of public attention through popular books and articles in periodicals.[35] But social psychology is currently undergoing a deep crisis influenced by mistakes, poor scientific practise, rushed conclusions, and the career aspirations of many rather than the thoughtful, scientific truth-finding of all.

The crisis goes back to the late 1960s, when attempts to improve social psychology had failed.[36] And the crisis was perpetuated with greater force about nine years ago, when it became more and more apparent that many of psychology's studies and propositions are highly flawed, or simply false.[37] One could

---

[34] H. Ebbinghaus quoted in Hans J. Eysenck, *Decline & Fall of the Freudian Empire* (London: Routledge, 1985), 34–35.
[35] https://www.britannica.com/science/social-psychology. Accessed August 23, 2023.
[36] Ian Parker, *The Crisis in Modern Social Psychology and How to End It* (London: Routledge, 2014 (1989)).
[37] Stuart Ritchie writes about the replication crisis in general: "So how have we reached the point where an incendiary title like 'Why Most Published Research Findings Are False' seems not like an absurd overstatement but a reasonable proposition?" See: Stuart Ritchie, *Science Fictions: Exposing Fraud, Bias, Negligence, and Hype in Science* (New York: Vintage, 2020), 17; See also: J. P. A. Ioannidis, "Correction: Why Most Published Research Findings Are False," *PLOS Medicine* 19.8 (2020): e1004085. https://doi.org/10.1371/journal.pmed.1004085. Other scholars use the term "false" as well to make their particular arguments. See for instance: J. P. Simmons, L. D. Nelson, and U. Simonsohn, "False-positive psychology: undisclosed flexibility in data collection and analysis allows presenting anything as significant," *Psychol. Sci.* 22 (2011): 1359–1366. doi: 10.1177/0956797611417632; G. Francis, "The psychology of replication and replication in psychology," *Perspect. Psychol. Sci.* 7 (2012): 585–594. doi: 10.1177/1745691612459520 ("experimental replication is the final arbiter in determining whether effects are true or false;" 585); B. D. Earp and D. Trafimow, "Replication, falsification, and the crisis of confidence in social psychology," *Front. Psychol.* 6 (2015): 621. doi: 10.3389/fpsyg.2015.00621. In regard to science in general, see Charles Darwin (*Descent of Man*, (Appleton, NY: American Home Library Co., 1871, 780): "False facts are highly injurious to the progress of science, for they often endure long; but false views, if sup-

argue that the most crucial moment was in 2010, when Cornell psychologist Daryl Bem published a study in *The Journal of Personality and Social Psychology*.[38] His study was based on accepted experimental methods but claimed to have found evidence for humans being able to perceive the future. As psychologist Eric-Jan Wagenmakers et al. concluded in a response to Bem's paper: "Our assessment suggests that something is deeply wrong with the way experimental psychologists design their studies and report their statistical results."[39] Or in 2012, when Yale University's John Bargh published a much-heralded 1996 study[40] that purported that reading about old people made people walk more slowly; the study could not be replicated,[41] despite its having been widely accepted and cited more than 6,300 times.[42] Influential textbook findings in psychology such as the so-called "marshmallow test,"[43] or Daniel Kahneman's "priming" effect, haven't been able to withstand the crisis either. In his 2011 best-seller *Thinking, Fast and Slow*, the Nobel prize-winning psychologist wrote about priming: "Disbelief is not an option. The results are not made up, nor are they statistical flukes. You have no

---

ported by some evidence, do little harm, for everyone takes a salutary pleasure in proving their falseness," quoted in Peter McDonald, *The Oxford Dictionary of Medical Quotations* (Oxford: Oxford University Press, 2004), 28; Karl Popper (*Conjectures and Refutations: The Growth of Scientific Knowledge* (London: Routledge, 1963), 36): "The criterion of the scientific status of a theory is its falsifiability, or refutability, or testability." Quoted by the American Psychological Association on https://blog.apastyle.org/apastyle/2009/11/the-three-rs-of-apa-style-part-2.html. Accessed August 23, 2023.

38 D. J. Bem, "Feeling the future: Experimental evidence for anomalous retroactive influences on cognition and affect," *Journal of Personality and Social Psychology* 100 (2011): 407–425. doi:10.1037/a0021524.

39 E.-J. Wagenmakers, R. Wetzels, D. Borsboom, and H. L. J. van der Maas, "Why psychologists must change the way they analyse their data: The case of psi," Comment on Bem (2011): 426, http://dx.doi.org/10.1037/a0022790. For a reply by Bem, see: https://www.alice.id.tue.nl/references/bem-et-al-2011.pdf. Accessed August 23, 2023.

40 J. A. Bargh, M. Chen, and L. Burrows, "Automaticity of social behavior: Direct effects of trait construct and stereotype activation on action," *Journal of Personality and Social Psychology* 71.2 (1996): 230–244. https://doi.org/10.1037/0022-3514.71.2.230.

41 S. Doyen, O. Klein, C.-L. Pichon, and A. Cleeremans, "Behavioral Priming: It's All in the Mind, but Whose Mind?" *PLoS ONE* 7.1 (2012): e29081. https://doi.org/10.1371/journal.pone.0029081. Accessed August 23, 2023.

42 From Google Scholar as of April 2023. See also: Stuart Ritchie, *Science Fictions: Exposing Fraud, Bias, Negligence, and Hype in Science* (New York: Vintage 2020), Part II – Faults and Flaws, 6. Hype.

43 T. W. Watts, G. J. Duncan, and H. Quan, "Revisiting the Marshmallow Test: A Conceptual Replication Investigating Links Between Early Delay of Gratification and Later Outcomes," *Psychological Science* 29.7 (2018): 1159–1177.

choice but to accept that the major conclusions of these studies are true."[44] Just a year later, Kahneman warned in an open letter that despite him being a "general believer" in priming, "a train wreck" was approaching the concept.[45]

The once highly respected social psychologist Diederik Alexander Stapel, who taught at Tilburg University in the Netherlands, had to retract 58 of his fraudulent publications (as of 2019). *The New York Times* called him "perhaps the biggest con man in academic science."[46] Stapel received quite a lot of media attention for his scientifically unbacked claims that "a trash-filled environment tended to bring out racist tendencies in individuals" and "media attention for a study indicating that eating meat made people selfish and less social."[47]

Unsurprisingly, critique is coming from all kinds of sides within academia and the public calling social psychology basically a dead field. Clinical psychologist Jordan B. Peterson has described social psychology as fundamentally a "corrupt enterprise" of appalling methods, which come up with categories that do not exist and lead to a "pollution" of the literature.[48] A quote by Noam Chomsky from 1988 might be brought to mind here as well: "It is quite possible – overwhelmingly probable, one might guess – that we will always learn more about human life and human personality from novels than from scientific psychology."[49]

But of course, there are also examples of literature portraying human nature completely wrong and even in contradiction to real-life events. *The Lord of the Flies* is a striking example.[50] And in general, the truth of literature is not the truth of science that relies on testable generalizations of universal validity. Maybe Proust and Goethe knew more about human nature than any psychologist, but their truth remains partial. We do, hence, rely on science.

What have been considered scientific findings in social psychology were mostly no more than good guesses at best. "It's likely," wrote the *Chronicle of Higher Education* in regard to social psychology, "that many, perhaps most, of the

---

[44] Daniel Kahneman, *Thinking, Fast and Slow* (New York: Penguin Books 2012), 57.
[45] https://www.nature.com/articles/d41586-019-03755-2. Accessed August 23, 2023.
[46] https://www.nytimes.com/2013/04/28/magazine/diederik-stapels-audacious-academic-fraud.html. Accessed August 23, 2023.
[47] https://www.nytimes.com/2013/04/28/magazine/diederik-stapels-audacious-academic-fraud.html. Accessed August 23, 2023.
[48] https://www.youtube.com/watch?v=ZOfbRF48tcA. Accessed August 23, 2023. https://www.youtube.com/watch?v=wEdBgRWkF-I. Accessed August 23, 2023.
[49] Noam Chomsky, *Language and Problems of Knowledge: The Managua Lectures* (Cambridge, MA: MIT Press, 1998), 159 (Lecture 5).
[50] https://www.theguardian.com/books/2020/may/09/the-real-lord-of-the-flies-what-happened-when-six-boys-were-shipwrecked-for-15-months. Accessed August 23, 2023.

studies published in the past couple of decades are flawed."[51] And "If you're a psychologist who has built a career on what may turn out to be a mirage, it's genuinely terrifying."[52] "Our literature is packed with unreliable findings," according to Steve Lindsay, professor of psychology at the University of Victoria and editor of *Psychological Science*. "And I can imagine if you hitched your whole wagon to a concept that doesn't seem to be a real thing, that could be threatening."[53]

Of course, people should not begin to mistrust science in general by overblowing the replication crisis or portraying it as proof of science overall being false or corrupt. But, since social psychologists working on antisemitism, the Holocaust, and anti-Zionism largely ignore the crisis all together, the field is in need of an honest exploration, which I seek to present here. I am not aware of many social psychologists rescinding their published studies on these subjects, despite the depth of the replication crisis. Even worse, one continues to see unverifiable findings from social psychology inserted into Jewish studies. To ignore this crisis until it somehow goes away is harmful to the field, in my view. Rather, we need to rethink how to deal with these flawed "findings," so that other scientists no longer borrow from them. Otherwise, one discipline's crisis will affect the other as erroneous research is blindly brought into the field of antisemitism studies.

The "pollution" of the literature is apparent in pre-crisis literature, such as the 2002 book *Understanding Genocide: The Social Psychology of the Holocaust* (edited by Leonard S. Newman and Ralph Erber),[54] which relies heavily on studies now known to be flawed. But we should be more concerned that some scholars still incorporate invalid conclusions into the study of antisemitism and thus further pollute the literature and the public understanding despite the crisis.

In her 2012 TED Talk,[55] social psychologist and former faculty member of Harvard Business School, Amy Cuddy, introduced the idea of "power posing" to the wider public. Her TED Talk became at some point the second most watched TED talk ever,[56] and her following book, *Presence: Bringing Your Boldest Self to Your Biggest Challenges,* a *New York Times* bestseller. Power posing can be described

---

51 https://www.chronicle.com/article/i-want-to-burn-things-to-the-ground/. Accessed August 23, 2023.
52 https://www.chronicle.com/article/i-want-to-burn-things-to-the-ground/. Accessed August 23, 2023.
53 https://www.chronicle.com/article/i-want-to-burn-things-to-the-ground/. Accessed August 23, 2023.
54 Leonard S. Newman and Ralph Erber, eds., *Understanding Genocide: The Social Psychology of the Holocaust* (Oxford: Oxford University Press, 2002).
55 Amy Cuddy, "Your body language may shape who you are," *TED* Talk (June 2012). Retrieved 6 July 2019. (The talk was originally titled "Your Body Language Shapes Who You Are").
56 Ritchie, *Science Fictions*, 29.

as a self-improvement technique: the claim is that standing with legs apart for two minutes like superman or wonder woman, Oprah or Mick Jagger, increases testosterone, decreases cortisol, and makes one perform better at job interviews due to an increase of confidence. The media reported quite a bit about this fascinating idea, with the *New York Times* enthusiastically summarizing: "If you act powerfully, you will begin to think powerfully."[57] Unfortunately, Cuddy and her colleagues' research could not be replicated,[58] one of her original research partners coming to the conclusion that: "I do not believe that 'power pose effects' are real . . . the evidence against the existence of power poses is undeniable."[59] Since then, power posing is often cited as an example of the replication crisis.[60]

This, however, did not keep Cuddy from making similarly bold and scientifically-unbacked claims about antisemitism in a *New York Times*[61] article in November 2018, or so it seems to me. "The Psychology of Anti-Semitism: Why is prejudice against Jewish people so often expressed in sudden waves of virulent, even exterminatory attacks?" states:

> To better understand the various ways in which bigotry manifests, the psychologists Susan Fiske, Peter Glick and I developed a new theory of prejudice, one that focuses on the content of stereotypes of out-groups. We have found that how an out-group is stereotyped predicts how the prejudice against it gets expressed. This theory — tested over more than 20 years

---

57 David Brooks, "Matter Over Mind," *The New York Times* (20 April 2011).
58 E. Ranehill, A. Dreber, M. Johannesson, S. Leiberg, S. Sul, and R. A. Weber, "Assessing the Robustness of Power Posing: No Effect on Hormones and Risk Tolerance in a Large Sample of Men and Women," *Psychological Science* 26.5 (2015): 653–656. doi:10.1177/0956797614553946; Katie E. Garrison, David Tang, and Brandon J. Schmeichel, "Embodying Power," *Social Psychological and Personality Science* 7.7 (2016): 623–630.
59 Jesse Singal, "'Power Posing' Co-author: 'I Do Not Believe That 'Power Pose' Effects Are Real,'" *New York Magazine* (26 September 2016). See https://faculty.haas.berkeley.edu/dana_carney/pdf_my%20position%20on%20power%20poses.pdf. Accessed August 23, 2023.

Regarding Cuddy's response, see: https://www.thecut.com/2016/09/read-amy-cuddys-response-to-power-posing-critiques.html; https://www.nytimes.com/2017/10/18/magazine/when-the-revolution-came-for-amy-cuddy.html. Accessed August 23, 2023.
60 Tracy King, "Sajid Javid and the strange science behind power poses," *The Guardian* (1 May 2018); Jesse Singal, "How Should We Talk About Amy Cuddy, Death Threats, and the Replication Crisis?" *New York Magazine* (25 April 2017); Jesse Singal, "There's an Interesting House-of-Cards Element to the Fall of Power Poses," *New York Magazine* (27 September 2016); Andrew Gelman and Kaiser Fung, "'The Power of the "Power Pose': Amy Cuddy's famous finding is the latest example of scientific overreach," *Slate* (19 January 2016); https://slate.com/technology/2016/01/amy-cuddys-power-pose-research-is-the-latest-example-of-scientific-overreach.html. Accessed August 23, 2023.
61 https://www.nytimes.com/2018/11/03/opinion/sunday/psychology-anti-semitism.html. Accessed August 23, 2023.

by us and others in hundreds of studies, with tens of thousands of participants, across many cultures — helps explain why anti-Semitism often erupts in such violent bursts.

By leaving other theories of antisemitism unmentioned in her article, Cuddy presents her discoveries – again – as if she has come up with a powerful new idea that boldly explains it all: the Holocaust, the Tree of Life Synagogue massacre in Pittsburgh, genocide in Cambodia, everything explained in one simple new theory of prejudice she developed with Glick and Fiske that helps us to understand why violence often erupts. Tellingly, Andrew Gelman, professor of statistics and political science at Columbia University, wrote of Fiske and Cuddy's research on elderly stereotypes, which they conducted with Michael I. Norton,[62] that it would be "riddled through with errors," "unpublishable," and

> when the errors were pointed out to them, they refused to reconsider anything . . . For Cuddy, Norton, and Fiske to step back and think that maybe almost everything they've been doing for years is all a mistake . . . they'll probably never take it . . . Fiske and her friends and students followed a certain path which has given them fame, fortune, and acclaim. Question the path, and you question the legitimacy of all that came from it. And that can't be pleasant.[63]

Fiske, on the other hand, has responded harshly to her critics as "methodological terrorists" and "self-appointed data police."[64] Criticism, moreover, should only be expressed "in private, in respected journals, or not at all."[65] Yet any simple explanation of human behavior, be it prejudice or any other form of human action, does not suffice. Anyone who is not confused by the human mind has not understood it. And arguably, "prejudice" does not even exist as a category that is inde-

---

[62] Amy J. C. Cuddy, Michael I. Norton, and Susan T. Fiske, "This Old Stereotype: The Pervasiveness and Persistence of the Elderly Stereotype," *Journal of Social Issues* 61.2 (2005): 267–285.
[63] Andrew Gelman, "What has happened down here is the winds have changed," blog post (21 September 2016): https://statmodeling.stat.columbia.edu/2016/09/21/what-has-happened-down-here-is-the-winds-have-changed/. While Gelman is recorded as stating later on in the article that "I'm not saying that none of Fiske's work would replicate or that most of it won't replicate or even that a third of it won't replicate," on his personal blog "Cuddy's name, far from the only one he repeatedly invoked, became a go-to synecdoche for faulty science writ large," according to Susan Dominus, "When the Revolution Came for Amy Cuddy," *The New York Times Magazine* (18 October 2017). See https://www.nytimes.com/2017/10/18/magazine/when-the-revolution-came-for-amy-cuddy.html; Accessed August 23, 2023. See also Gelman and Fung, "'The Power of the "Power Pose"', *Slate* (19 January 2016).
[64] Rafi Letzter, "Scientists are furious after a famous psychologist accused her peers of 'methodological terrorism,'" *Business Insider* (22 September 2016). https://www.businessinsider.com/susan-fiske-methodological-terrorism-2016-9?r=US&IR=T. Accessed 23, 2023.
[65] Letzter, "Scientists are furious," *Business Insider* (22 September 2016).

pendent of social and historical context. There is no natural history of "prejudice" as a mental disfunction a psychologist could discover and explain; there is only the social history of a terrible phenomenon.

Understanding the replication crisis is especially important because psychological research on antisemitism often finds prominent resonance in the media, while a wider audience might not be able to distinguish its results as guesses, not verifiable academic findings. An example of this is, in my view, Glenn Geher's contribution to *Psychology Today* called "The Evolutionary Psychology of Antisemitism".[66] Geher is professor of psychology at the State University of New York at New Paltz and founding director of the campus' Evolutionary Studies (EvoS) program. Evolutionary psychology is "the study of behaviour, thought, and feeling as viewed through the lens of evolutionary biology. Evolutionary psychologists presume all human behaviours reflect the influence of physical and psychological predispositions that helped human ancestors survive and reproduce."[67] Evolutionary psychology has received significant criticism.[68] Critics argue that the field could predict all human behaviours, including contradictory ones. "It has no scientific value," writes the mathematician and philosopher David Berlinski about evolutionary psychology, "We might as well be honest with one another. It has no value whatsoever."[69] Or, in the words of Noam Chomsky: "You find that people cooperate, you say, 'Yeah, that contributes to their genes' perpetuating. You find that they fight, you say, 'Sure, that's obvious, because it means that their genes perpetuate and not somebody else's.' In fact, just about anything you find, you can make up some story for it."[70] (And a danger also lies in evolutionary psychology being misused to argue for antisemitic ideas.[71])

---

[66] https://www.psychologytoday.com/us/blog/darwins-subterranean-world/201804/the-evolutionary-psychology-anti-semitism. Accessed August 23, 2023.
[67] https://www.britannica.com/science/evolutionary-psychology. Accessed August 23, 2023.
[68] See for instance: Daniel L. Schacter, Daniel Wegner, and Daniel Gilbert, *Psychology* (New York: Worth, 2007), 26–27.
[69] David Berlinski, *The Devil's Delusion: Atheism and Its Scientific Pretensions* (2nd ed.; New York: Basic Books, 2009), 168.
[70] John Horgan, *The Undiscovered Mind: How the Brain Defies Explanation* (London: Phoenix, 2000), 179.
[71] Kevin MacDonald was professor of evolutionary psychology at California State University, Long Beach and the author of *A People That Shall Dwell Alone: Judaism as a Group Evolutionary Strategy* and *The Culture of Critique: An Evolutionary Analysis of Jewish Involvement in Twentieth-Century Intellectual and Political Movements*. He has been called to testify for David Irving in his trail against Penguin Books and Deborah Lipstadt, who had called Irving out for his Holocaust denial. *Slate* wrote that MacDonald's "ideas about Jews have almost no relevance to the case but represent the broadest, ugliest, and most vicious anti-Semitism passing for scholarship in this country today . . . MacDonald's central thesis is that Judaism is best understood not as a

Stanley Milgram was one of the most important figures in social psychology and famous for his experiments on obedience. In his article Geher notes about him: "Stanley Milgram, another American Jew, showed that any regular Joe is capable of obeying an authority figure to the point of being able to kill an innocent other."[72] This is wrong. Science writer Gina Perry has investigated Milgram's data, for which she received much international acclaim.[73] Her research suggests that Milgram had in fact manipulated his results and that there was a "troubling mismatch between (published) descriptions of the experiment and evidence of what actually transpired," since "only half of the people who undertook the experiment fully believed it was real and of those, 66% disobeyed the experimenter."[74] This, she finds, is "an

---

religion but as a blueprint for an experiment in eugenics–a 'group evolutionary strategy,' he calls it–designed to maximize a single trait: intelligence." See: https://slate.com/news-and-politics/2000/01/evolutionary-psychology-s-anti-semite.html. Accessed August 23, 2023. And the Anti-Defamation League writes that: "Kevin MacDonald is an anti-Semitic tenured professor of evolutionary psychology at California State University, Long Beach (CSULB), where he has worked since 1985. MacDonald's anti-Semitic views became widely known after he wrote a series of books on Jews, starting in the mid-1990s. In these works, he argued that Jews are a hostile elite in American society who undermine the country's European heritage and traditions in an effort to destroy Europeans. Couching his views as legitimate intellectual inquiry, MacDonald has asserted that anti-Semitism, including the anti-Jewish hatred exhibited by the Nazis and those who carried out the Spanish Inquisition, is a 'rational' response to Judaism." See: https://www.adl.org/resources/news/kevin-macdonald. Accessed August 23, 2023. This, of course, does not reflect the entire field, and MacDonald's work has long been ignored by mainstream evolutionary psychologists. It seems, therefore, disturbing to me that *Evolutionary Psychological Science* (a Springer Nature journal) published a defence of his work in 2019 with a paper entitled "Jewish Group Evolutionary Strategy Is the Most Plausible Hypothesis." See E. Dutton "Jewish Group Evolutionary Strategy Is the Most Plausible Hypothesis: a Response to Nathan Cofnas' Critical Analysis of Kevin MacDonald's Theory of Jewish Involvement in Twentieth Century Ideological Movements," *Evolutionary Psychological Science* 5 (2019): 136–142. https://doi.org/10.1007/s40806-018-0158-4. Accessed August 23, 2023.

72 https://www.psychologytoday.com/us/blog/darwins-subterranean-world/201804/the-evolutionary-psychology-anti-semitism. Accessed August 23, 2023.

73 For instance, the Silver World Medal for a history documentary at the 2009 New York Festivals radio awards. See: http://www.gina-perry.com/about-gina/. Accessed August 23, 2023.

74 Gina Perry, *Behind the Shock Machine: the untold story of the notorious Milgram psychology experiments* (New York: The New Press, 2013). See also: Gina Perry et al., "Credibility and Incredulity in Milgram's Obedience Experiments: A Reanalysis of an Unpublished Test," *Social Psychology Quarterly* 83.1 (2019): 88–106; See also Johannes Lichtman, "Psych, Lies, and Audiotape: The Tarnished Legacy of the Milgram Shock Experiments," *Los Angeles Review of Books* (30 October 2013) https://lareviewofbooks.org/article/psych-lies-and-audiotape-the-tarnished-legacy-of-the-milgram-shock-experiments/ (accessed August 23, 2023): ". . . to what extent can we trust his raw data in the first place? In her riveting new book, *Behind the Shock Machine: The Untold Story of the Notorious Milgram Psychology Experiments*, Australian psychologist Gina Perry tackles this

unexpected outcome" that "leaves social psychology in a difficult situation."[75] Similarly, James Waller, chair of Holocaust and Genocide Studies at Keene State College, convincingly demonstrates that Milgram's experiments "do not correspond well" to genocide and mass killings, because the entire study only lasted for about an hour, because the subjects had no previous exposure to their victims, and because of the overreaching institution behind the experiment, which assured that there would be no permanent damage done to victims in the experiment.[76]

Geher also relies in his argument on the research of Philip Zimbardo, who became world-famous with his "Stanford Prison Experiment," which pretended to demonstrate the power of situation over human behaviour. Unfortunately – or fortunately, one must say – the Stanford Prison Experiment was flawed. Thibault Le Texier demonstrates via transcripts of tapes of Zimbardo that he was "intervening directly in the experiment, giving his 'guards' very precise instructions on how to behave – going as far as to suggest specific ways of dehumanising the prisoners, like denying them the use of toilets."[77] Stuart Ritchie, a psychologist at King's College London, called Zimbardo's experiment, therefore, a "heavily stage-managed production" and "scientifically meaningless."[78] Geher also relies on Asch's research on conformity. Augustine Brannigan, however, sees Asch, despite his prominent place in social psychology courses and textbooks, as offering "among the least compelling evidence for the successful utilization of experimental methodology."[79] Further, "Asch's entire orientation appears to have little relevance to everyday life . . . [his] experiment tells us nothing informative about the process of propaganda during World War II. It says nothing about genocide and the political use of scapegoats to misattribute the real misery of German society during the thirties. It says nothing about national animosities, nor the state's legitimation of violence to deal with opponents."[80] Geher, however, concludes in his publication on antisemitism

---

very topic, taking nothing for granted. Her chilling investigation of the experiments and their aftereffects suggests that Milgram manipulated results, misled the public, and flat out lied in order to deflect criticism and further the thesis for which he would become famous: that the Holocaust could have happened in New Haven."
75 Gina Perry, "Taking A Closer Look At Milgram's Shocking Obedience Study," interview on "All Things Considered," NPR (28 August 2013).
76 James Waller, *Becoming Evil: How Ordinary People Commit Genocide and Mass Killing* (Oxford: Oxford University Press, 2007), 111–113.
77 Ritchie, *Science Fictions*, 30.
78 Ritchie, *Science Fictions*, 30.
79 Augustine Brannigan, *The Rise and Fall of Social Psychology: The Use and Misuse of the Experimental Method* (London: Routledge, 2017), 33.
80 Brannigan, *Rise and Fall*, 49.

> Look, I know that this post deals with very dark content. But the human condition is often very dark and we cannot turn a blind eye. It is up to us, the concerned citizens of the world now, to make sure that something like the Holocaust never happens again. If we want to help make for a better future, then we need to understand the past. And we need to understand the social science that helps us map out exactly what went wrong in the past so that we are equipped to make for a better future. We ignore the social and behavioral science on the topic of hate to our own peril.[81]

But Geher does not provide much reliable science for his bold claims as far as I can tell. He communicates his ideas on the psychology of antisemitism to the wider public as reliable science, which it is not. It might be a good guess, an interesting thought, enjoyable to read as far as the topic allows, but it is not a scientific conclusion, and certainly not *the* explanation of antisemitism.

Florette Cohen Abady's 2019 publication, "The Psychology of Modern Antisemitism: Theory, Research, and Methodology,"[82] is another unfortunate example of unverifiable social psychology findings that still find their way into the field of antisemitism studies. Cohen Abady is associate professor for social psychology at CUNY College of Staten Island. Her publication does not mention the replication crisis of recent years while she builds on the field of social psychology to develop her theory of antisemitism, a theory that relies heavily on social-psychology claims concerning in-group bias and stereotypes: "According to Henri Tajfel, in-group bias is psychologically motivated by the need for self-esteem."[83] Yet "self-esteem" as a psychological category, rather than as a lifestyle term of the human potential movement of Ayn Rand and the like, has become a shaky concept considering the many flawed studies associated with it.[84] Self-esteem is certainly an easy idea to fix all kinds of problems from addictions to crime, poor classroom performance, teenage pregnancies, and antisemitism. Problems are made simply to float away with the right mindset adjustment. The too-easy nature of boosting self-esteem as a method becomes particularly evident in the American educa-

---

[81] https://www.psychologytoday.com/us/blog/darwins-subterranean-world/201804/the-evolutionary-psychology-anti-semitism. Accessed August 23, 2023.
[82] Florette Cohen Abady, "The Psychology of Modern Antisemitism: Theory, Research, and Methodology," in Armin Lange, Kerstin Mayerhofer, Dinat Porat, and Lawrence H. Schiffman (eds.), *Comprehending and Confronting Antisemitism: A Multifaceted Approach* (Berlin: De Gruyter, 2020) 271–296.
[83] Cohen Abady, "The Psychology of Modern Antisemitism," 276.
[84] Roy F. Baumeister et al., "Exploding the Self-Esteem Myth," *Scientific American* (December 2005); scientificamerican.com/article/exploding-the-self-esteem-2005-12; Roy F. Baumeister et al., "Does High Self-Esteem Cause Better Performance, Interpersonal Success, Happiness, or Healthier Lifestyles?" *Psychological Science in the Public Interest* 4.1 (2003): 1–44, doi.org/10.1111/1529–1006.01431; Jesse Sigal, *The Quick Fix: Why Fad Psychology Can't Cure Our Social Ills* (New York: Farrar, Straus & Giroux, 2021).

tional system: there "It became a surrogate for the stuff that might actually have done some good,"[85] such as spending money on teachers, notes Steve Salero. But even if the idea does have value, I do not know of any convincing evidence that antisemites have particularly low self-esteem. Criminals generally, in fact, have been found to have higher levels of self-esteem.[86]

Wouldn't it be marvellous to find that XY leads to antisemitism and that by eliminating XY we could get rid of the problem? But the simplistic idea that "in-group bias is psychologically motivated by the need for self-esteem" ignores a classic problem in science: A may cause B, but so could B cause A. In fact, what self-esteem advocates ignore, writes mathematical psychologist Robyn M. Dawes, is "the simple principle that much of our feeling results from what we do rather than causing us to do it."[87]

A former president of the American Psychological Association (APA) stated in 1988: "We are all teachers. I think my clients see me as primarily a teacher. We have taught the whole culture . . . Our job is to bring knowledge to the world."[88] But what do self-esteem advocates among psychologists have to teach? A belief system, an ideology, a philosophy of life perhaps? Ultimately, they teach (or preach) a way of thinking about us in this world in terms of everybody's obligation to increase their own mental health, to boost wellbeing by maximizing self-esteem. The psychologists Shelley Taylor, for instance, claims to have discovered that self-esteem is even more important than realism: "Every theory of mental health," she states, "considers a positive self-concept to be the cornerstone of a healthy ego."[89] Following this ill-guided train of thought, a person who does not think well of himself or herself would be a failure, and a narcissist would be of good mental health. This ignores the fundamental fact that not all emotional suffering is bad; otherwise we would all be psychopaths. Suffering can also lead to more maturity and understanding – something the self-esteem branch of psychology gets so horribly wrong while they preach their toxic ideology to vast parts of society. And considering that it would be of value, I wonder who would determine if one has too little or too much self-esteem, if not other people, as that de-

---

[85] Steve Salero, *Sham: How the Self-Help Movement Made America Helpless* (New York: Crown Forum, 2005).
[86] Will Storr, "The Man Who Destroyed America's Ego," *Matter* (blog), Medium (25 February 2014). medium.com/matter/the-man-who-destroyed-americas-ego-94d214257b5. Accessed August 23, 2023.
[87] Robyn M. Dawes, *House of Cards: Psychology and Psychotherapy Built on Myth* (New York: The Free Press, 1996), 10.
[88] K. Fisher, "Graham: 'A Product of My Times,'" *The APA Monitor* 19 (1988): 5.
[89] Shelley Taylor, *Positive Illusions: Creative Self-Deception and the Healthy Mind* (New York: Basic Books, 1989), 227.

termination cannot come from oneself. Hence, it is more a moral judgement and cultural category than science, which needs to be free of moral judgement. It is simply not a category that can be scientifically observed.

It is a mistake, common especially among American psychologists, to overemphasize the individual self without any societal context. The Israeli social psychologist Daniel Bar-Tal put it well in 2019:

> I still have the feeling that social psychology in general does not fulfil its promise as it was shaped by its founding fathers. They considered the study of macrosocietal context as part of the endeavor of social psychology during the 1930s through the early 1950s. But during the 1960s, the mainstream of social psychology, especially the American wing, gravitated toward psychological-individualistic orientation with major reliance on experimentation. With some shifts, this is still the dominant trend . . . Without such focus, social psychology fails, as a study of human social behavior, to understand key facets of human behaviour.[90]

In her argument about antisemitism Cohen Abady also relies on terror-management theory (TMT),[91] whose claims also can't be replicated, as recent research has found.[92] Yet she writes: "TMT provides a straightforward explanation for antisemitism."[93] Again, one gets the unfortunate impression of an unscientific tendency toward straightforward, powerful explanations on the part of many social psychologists. Cohen Abady, moreover, writes that "More recent research replicated these find-

---

[90] Daniel Bar-Tal, "The Challenges of Social and Political Psychology in Pursuit of Peace: Personal Account," *Peace and Conflict: Journal of Peace Psychology* 25.3 (2019): 187.
[91] Cohen Abady, "The Psychology of Modern Antisemitism," 278.
[92] J. Rodríguez-Ferreiro, I. Barberia, J. González-Guerra, and M. A. Vadillo, "Are we truly special and unique? A replication of Goldenberg et al. (2001)," *R Soc Open Sci.* 6 (2019): 191114. doi: 10.1098/rsos.191114; Richard Klein et al., "Many Labs 4: Failure to Replicate Mortality Salience Effect With and Without Original Author Involvement," *PsyArXiv* (11 December 2019); https://www.cos.io/blog/many-labs-4-failure-replicate-mortality-salience-effect-and-without-original-author-involvement; accessed August 23, 2023; Lihan Chen, Rachele Benjamin, Addison Lai, and Steven Heine. "Managing the Terror of Publication Bias: A Comprehensive P-curve Analysis of the Terror Management Theory Literature," *PsyArXiv* (3 January 2022); doi:10.31234/osf.io/kuhy6; https://replicationindex.com/2022/02/13/rr22-terror-management/; https://replicationindex.com/2022/02/13/rr22-terror-management/; accessed August 23, 2023. For other critiques on terror-management theory, see for instance: Lee A. Kirkpatrick and Carlos David Navarrete, "Reports of My Death Anxiety Have Been Greatly Exaggerated: A Critique of Terror Management Theory from an Evolutionary Perspective," *Psychological Inquiry* 17.4 (2006): 288–298; Carlos David Navarrete and Daniel M. T. Fessel, "Normative Bias and Adaptive Challenges: A Relational Approach to Coalitional Psychology and a Critique of Terror Management Theory," *Evolutionary Psychology* 3.1 (2005). https://doi.org/10.1177/147470490500300121.
[93] Cohen Abady, "The Psychology of Modern Antisemitism," 278.

ings"[94] in reference to a 2009 study.[95] However, a vividly discussed study published in 2019 (and announced in 2017) by over 30 established scholars has found this not to be the case.[96] But let us assume for a moment that there is no replication crisis and that Cohen Abady's findings are grounded in scientific facts. What is the theory on antisemitism she comes up with? She argues for the disturbing idea that "antisemitism is, in part, a defense aimed at repressing death related anxieties."[97] Again: a "defense aimed at repressing death related anxieties," as if antisemites need help because they suffer from anxiety. Scientists should be free in their thinking and allowed to make mistakes, but the killing of six million Jews, the rejection of a job applicant for being Jewish, or lies about "the Jews", are clearly not acts of "defense," not even a little bit.

Robert Eisen's *Judaism and Violence: A Historical Analysis with Insights from Social Psychology*[98] is a book that still – in the year 2021 – relied in my estimation on pseudo-scientific findings of social psychology, especially Social Identity Theory and its emphasis on self-esteem. It is certainly possible to speak of violence within Judaism or by Jews (as it is of any other religion or people), but given the problem of antisemitism, it would have been more thoughtful to ground any study of it on actual science. Nor is the Israel-Palestine conflict, as argued, a self-esteem question.

From 2012 to 2015, the German government has spent through the rather controversial[99] funding organization DFG over 120,000 Euros on a project to "empiri-

---

94 Cohen Abady, "The Psychology of Modern Antisemitism," 279.
95 Cf. F. Cohen, L. Jussim, K. D. Harber, and G. Bhasin, "Modern Anti-Semitism and Anti-Israeli Attitudes," *Journal of Personality and Social Psychology* 97.2 (2009): 290–306.
96 Klein et al., "Many Labs 4."
97 Cohen Abady, "The Psychology of Modern Antisemitism," 291.
98 Robert Eisen, *Judaism and Violence: A Historical Analysis with Insights from Social Psychology* (Cambridge: Cambridge University Press, 2021).
99 The DFG (German Research Foundation) is an institution designed for the promotion of science and research and funded by the German government. It has attracted important critique in my estimation: The legal scholar Volker Rieble and the literature scholar Roland Reuß criticised the organization's lack of transparency. A major newspaper in Germany, the *FAZ*, headlined their article with: "Freedom of Science is Threatened" (*Die freie Wissenschaft is bedroht*). See: https://www.faz.net/aktuell/feuilleton/forschung-und-lehre/kritik-an-der-dfg-die-freie-wissenschaft-ist-bedroht-11497511.html#Drucken; accessed August 23, 2023. Stefanie Salaw-Hanslmaier has argued that the DFG does not meet the requirement of the principles of democracy and the rule of law, see: Stefanie Salaw-Hanslmaier, *Die Rechtsnatur der Deutschen Forschungsgemeinschaft: Auswirkungen auf den Rechtsschutz des Antragstellers* (Hamburg: Verlag Dr. Kovač, 2003). This is something *Die Zeit*, another major newspaper in Germany, has reported on as well. See: https://www.zeit.de/studium/hochschule/2011-10/streit-dfg; accessed August 23, 2023. *Der Spiegel* reported about often relatively mild penalties for funded researchers by the DFG even in a case

cally examine which psychological processes underlie the phenomenon of secondary antisemitism." The results of a total of eight studies, however, "did not provide any indication of the validity of the assumption of experimentally verifiable secondary antisemitism."[100] But this has not led Roland Imhoff, a professor of Social and Legal Psychology who led the project, to question whether accepted psychological methods are able at all to produce any scientific knowledge on the phenomenon. Instead, it led him to "argue against the originally assumed effect of defensive antisemitism being robust."[101] Imhoff was – contrary to so many of his colleagues in the field – honest enough not to present unverifiable study results, which could have led to a publication. He simply didn't find out anything. Given the magnitude of the replication crisis, this is admirable. But how many costly studies does Germany need to figure out that antisemitism is a real thing and psychology a dead end?

Instead of backing down from unscientific and absurd guesses about the origins of antisemitism, some still seem to welcome social psychology, or even call to expand its funding. The Institute for the Study of Global Antisemitism (ISGAP) recently appointed retired psychology professor David Nussbaum as Senior Research

---

of years of gross neglect of duties and the manipulation of data. See: https://www.spiegel.de/wissenschaft/mensch/dfg-erteilt-immunologin-bulfone-paus-ruege-wegen-fehlverhaltens-a-871920.html. Accessed August 23, 2023; The DFG has also been criticised for funding a research project on "Jewish Pimps, Prostitutes and Campaigners in a Translational German and British Context, 1875–1940". The project is conducted by Stefanie Fischer-Wolff and Stefanie Schüler-Springorum (both Center for Research on Antisemitism, Technical University of Berlin) and Daniel Lee (University of Sheffield). Given the Nazi stereotype of the "Jewish pimp" and their defamation of Jews causing prostitution, at least the title and description of the project seem highly problematic to me, to say the least. While the project seeks "historical reappraisal" [*historischen Aufarbeitung*, a term usually used in German in the context of the Nazis or East German history] of Jews in the sex trade, it is a central concern for the research team to enter into a dialogue with the non-academic public. Unsurprisingly, German media has reported extremely critical about the project and the DFG for funding it. For the project description see: https://gepris.dfg.de/gepris/projekt/429039799?language=en; accessed September 10, 2023; https://gepris.dfg.de/gepris/projekt/429039799?language=de; accessed September 10, 2023. For a historical context see, for instance: Julia Roos, "Backlash against Prostitutes' Rights: Origins and Dynamics of Nazi Prostitution Policies," *Journal of the History of Sexuality* 11, no. 1/2 (2002): 79; For a critique in German media see: https://www.welt.de/kultur/plus207457329/Was-so-geforscht-wird-Juden-im-Sexhandel-oder-Ejaculatio-praecox.html; accessed September 10, 2023.

100 https://gepris.dfg.de/gepris/projekt/218311345?language=en&selectedSubTab=2; Accessed August 23, 2023. https://www.sozrepsy.uni-mainz.de/prof-dr-roland-imhoff/. Accessed August 23, 2023.

101 https://gepris.dfg.de/gepris/projekt/218311345?language=en&selectedSubTab=2. Accessed August 23, 2023.

Fellow.¹⁰² In an article about his new appointment for *ISGAP Flashpoint*, he wrote: "As a newly appointed ISGAP Senior Research Fellow and a psychologist, I was excited to begin exploring and adding to psychological insights in the study of antisemitism that earlier colleagues had discovered, with a particular emphasis on the last three decades."¹⁰³ While he tells of advances in the field beyond the work of Milgram, Zimbardo's Stanford Prison study, and others "it appears long past due for psychologists and psychology departments, and private and public granting agencies, to begin funding empirical psychological research on the various causes and sustaining forces of this oldest and unremitting hatred."¹⁰⁴

One gets the unfortunate impression that many social psychologists who deal with the issue of antisemitism prefer to ignore the crisis of their field all together, perhaps to survive in the "publish or perish" culture of academia, or maybe because they are true believers despite all evidence to the contrary. Rusi Jaspal is professor of psychology at Brighton University and board member of various so-

---

102 Among many highly respectable scholars at ISGAP one finds, unfortunately, other questionable engagements: Lihong Song, who sees Jewish studies in China as able to flourish because it is conducted by non-Jews, was appointed as research fellow there. See Song Lihong, "Reflections on Chinese Jewish Studies: A Comparative Perspective," in James Ross and Song Lihong (eds.), *The Image of Jews in Contemporary China* (Brookline, MA: Academic Studies Press, 2016), 209–210. The text in question reads as follows: "The modern scientific study of Jews and Judaism, from its beginnings in the *Wissenschaft des Judentums* to the present, is by and large Jewishly bound and fraught ... What looms largest behind these tensions and dilemmas is the intertwined nexus between critical Jewish learning and Jewish faith. In contrast, Chinese Jewish studies, produced – at least predominantly – by and for the Chinese, could be described as Jewish studies independent of Jewish faith and without an intent to cultivate and strengthen Jewish identity; hence Chinese Jewish studies is freed of the burden of searching of its role both in the academy and in the tradition of Jewish learning, a fate that even today's non-Jewish scholars of Jews and Judaism in Germany can hardly escape." Also, Meron Medzini has been invited to guest lecture at ISGAP despite publications of his which deny the genocidal nature of the Nanjing Massacre and Bulgaria's involvement in the Holocaust, his having called Franco's Spain a 'brave nation,' and his having advocated a conspiracy theory concerning 'certain anti-Semitic tendencies' (Steven Heine and María Sol Echarren, "Introduction," *Japan Studies Review* XXIII (2019)), wherein Jewish communities tend to 'open doors in the right places' in their home countries for Israel. See: https://isgap.org/tag/meron-medzini/; accessed August 23, 2023. For a critique see Schilling, "Japanese Studies in Israel," 143–154 and Schilling, "Review of *Under the Shadow of the Rising Sun*," 195–204.
103 https://isgap.org/flashpoint/where-is-the-psychology-of-antisemitism/#_ftnref1. Accessed August 23, 2023.
104 https://isgap.org/flashpoint/where-is-the-psychology-of-antisemitism/. Accessed September 27, 2023.

cial psychology journals[105] as well as *Israel Affairs*.[106] His book *Antisemitism and Anti-Zionism* uses social psychology as a framework.[107] His interest in the study of antisemitism is notable. Yet, in light of the replication crisis, the book can be read as a collection of interesting guesses perhaps, but arguably not as a report of scientific findings. Similarly, he relies on shaky ideas about self-esteem and stereotypes in his recent article "The social psychology of contemporary antisemitism," which he published in *Israel Affairs*.[108] I am not aware of Jaspal having retracted or revised any of his over 150 peer-reviewed articles and book chapters on social psychology of the past ten years and whether or not he should do so.[109] In my experience, scientific output usually starts with an idea one develops and discusses with colleagues, before funding gets sought, research conducted, the results put to paper, submitted to a journal, and peer-reviewed. For the past ten years, Jaspal has, based on the evidence I have seen, produced on average 1 peer-reviewed paper every four weeks (apart from his other academic obligations such as PhD supervision and journal board duties).[110] In 2022, Jaspal became Pro Vice-Chancellor for Research and Knowledge Exchange at the University of Brighton.[111] He has produced 23 peer-reviewed papers and two books in 2020 alone.[112] Maybe social psychology publications in general should not be compared to what other fields consider "scientific output"? Given the magnitude of the replication crisis, what he and so many of his colleagues in social psychology could do now is the most difficult and unsettling thing for any scientist: admit that the past decades of their research in social psychology were a waste of time, reject the entire structure their field stands on, and start again from scratch. This must be painfully difficult. But isn't it far better than sticking with an erroneous concept?

---

105 E.g., *European Journal of Social Psychology*; *Journal of Social and Political Psychology*.
106 *Israel Affairs*' official editorial board is listed incorrectly on its website (as of 18 March 2023). Michael Walzer told me that "to the best of his knowledge" he is not on the editorial board, as claimed by the journal. Others have told me that they do not have full online access to the journal's articles. Another listed member of the editorial board, David Vital, passed away in January 2023 at the age of 95. Nor is Howard Sachar still with us: he passed away in 2018 at the age of 90 but is still listed as an editorial board member. I do understand Jaspal to be an editorial board member because this is indicated on his website. See: https://www.rusijaspal.com/. Accessed August 23, 2023.
107 Rusi Jaspal, *Antisemitism and Anti-Zionism: Representation, Cognition and Everyday Talk* (London: Routledge, 2016). https://doi.org/10.4324/9781315567341.
108 Rusi Jaspal, "The social psychology of contemporary antisemitism," *Israel Affairs* 29 (2023): 31–51.
109 https://www.rusijaspal.com/publications. Accessed August 23, 2023.
110 https://www.rusijaspal.com/research. Accessed August 23, 2023; https://www.rusijaspal.com/Home. Accessed August 23, 2023.
111 https://www.rusijaspal.com/. Accessed August 23, 2023.
112 https://www.rusijaspal.com/publications. Accessed August 23, 2023.

Science should embrace failure and learn from it. The fact that this is not adequately happening in the field is not necessarily a sign of corruption, forgery, or an inability to practise science well, but "perhaps," as Theodore Dalrymple writes about people in general, "the desire for the illusion of understanding is generally greater than the desire for understanding itself."[113] This becomes particularly difficult when the media embraces big, "scientifically backed" ideas that might become false public knowledge. Such ideas are hard to put back into the bottle again once poured forth.

Despite any claims within the field of social psychology, there is no single, "straightforward explanation" for antisemitism. At least not yet. Science rarely produces anything straightforward, and we might even need to develop different theories of antisemitism for different cultural and historical settings. This is, of course, not to say that one form is less terrible than another. My argument is in kind, not in degree. I wonder, however, why the field of psychology doesn't see the replication crisis as an opportunity to rethink our knowledge about antisemitism, the Holocaust, or anti-Zionism. Are careers and academic prestige more important than admitting that an entire field is deeply flawed? Should we not debate what to do about the crisis before jumping to *the* new explanation with which social psychology presumably provides us?

It is intuitive to think that scientific progress is a linear, straightforward process, wherein every study adds some new knowledge. The replication crisis is a reminder that this is not the case. One should remain concerned with the continued, unquestioned presence of these "findings" in antisemitism, anti-Zionism, and Holocaust studies. Fortunately, psychology journals are currently getting better at demanding larger subject pools for the studies they publish, and they are more and more providing their peer-reviewers with open data in an attempt to heal the replication crisis. The field of antisemitism studies should follow suit by rejecting the results of unverifiable studies as foundational for understanding the phenomenon. Further, I suggest that the crisis should remind us to question the prominent standing in society of a deeply flawed field, namely social psychology, and that this is all the more important when it comes to public discourse and legislation surrounding Jew-hatred. "If we continue as we are," writes Chris Chambers so tellingly, "then psychology will diminish as a reputable science and could very well disappear. If we ignore the warning signs now, then in a hundred years or less, psychology may be regarded as one in a long line of quaint scholarly in-

---

113 Theodore Dalrymple, *Admirable Evasions* (New York: Encounter Books, 2020).

dulgences, much as we now regard alchemy or phrenology."[114] Chambers, himself a professor of cognitive neuroscience at the School of Psychology at Cardiff University, expects later generations to view psychology in general as protoscience, from an age when psychologists found themselves "trapped within a culture where the *appearance* of science was seen as an appropriate replacement for the *practice* of science."[115]

Ultimately, social psychology is a Potemkin Village of science. And it is one that finds excuses on the grounds of false "scientific" findings, which do not help to prevent, or even explain, antisemitism but rather help antisemites to evade personal responsibility.

---

[114] Chris Chambers, *The Seven Deadly Sins of Psychology: A Manifesto for Reforming the Culture of Scientific Practice* (Princeton: Princeton University Press, 2017), ix.
[115] Chambers, *The Seven Deadly Sins of Psychology*, ix.

Chapter II
Clinical Psychology

The individual is given much attention in clinical psychology, which is concerned with the diagnosis and treatment of mental disorders, for which clinical psychologists apply various types (alone or in combinations) of psychotherapy, such as psychoanalysis or behavioral therapy. They may also contribute to law courts in assessing the mental states of defendants or potential parolees (see the chapter on "Forensic Psychology"). Other clinical psychologists work in academic settings and are trained in experimental research and statistical procedures.[116]

Given the evidence, *p*-hacking (a practise where researchers exploit their degree of freedom to generate statistical significance) may very well be the norm in psychology.[117] The mathematician Aubrey Clayton goes even further and calls into question all psychological research due to a "fundamental misunderstanding of the quantification of uncertainty—that is, probability—and its role in drawing inferences from data."[118] While this is certainly true about social psychology, even clinical psychology increasingly seems to stand on shacky ground. Michael P. Hengartner, senior researcher in psychology at the Zurich University of Applied Sciences, argues that "inconsistent and systematically biased research findings persistently compromise the yield of clinical research."[119] In fact, the clinical psychological literature is often biased.[120] Such bias manifests as publication bias,[121]

---

[116] https://www.britannica.com/science/clinical-psychology. Accessed August 23, 2023.
[117] Chambers, *The Seven Deadly Sins of Psychology*, 29.
[118] Aubrey Clayton, *Bernoulli's Fallacy: Statistical Illogic and the Crisis of Modern Science* (New York: Columbia University Press, 2021), 1.
[119] Michael P. Hengartner, "Raising Awareness for the Replication Crisis in Clinical Psychology by Focusing on Inconsistencies in Psychotherapy Research: How Much Can We Rely on Published Findings from Efficacy Trials?" *Frontiers in psychology* 9 (2018); doi:10.3389/fpsyg.2018.00256.
[120] F. Leichsenring et al., "Biases in research: risk factors for non-replicability in psychotherapy and pharmacotherapy research," *Psychological Medicine* 47.6 (2017): 1000–1011.
[121] E. Driessen et al., "Does Publication Bias Inflate the Apparent Efficacy of Psychological Treatment for Major Depressive Disorder? A Systematic Review and Meta-Analysis of US National Institutes of Health-Funded Trials," *PLoS One* 10.9 (2015): e0137864.

allegiance bias,[122] sponsorship bias,[123] unblinded outcome assessors,[124] and small sample sizes.[125]

Even the most fundamental question of whether psychologists are able to diagnose mental illness is debated. David Rosenhan, a psychology professor at Stanford University, has demonstrated that "psychiatrists and nurses in four different hospitals could not distinguish patients deemed genuinely mentally ill from those who had initially faked their symptoms, to gain admission."[126] Rosenhan's findings were published in *Science*,[127] one of the world's top journals, in 1973. But the validity of his study has been questioned recently by Alison Abbott in *Nature*, another top journal, who reviewed *The Great Pretender*, a book on Rosenhan by Susannah Cahalan.[128]

Psychotherapy

Other scholars have pointed to the pseudo-scientific nature of psychotherapy and raised the point that its effects on depression may be entirely due to the placebo effect.[129] A look into the larger literature suggests, as well, that there is not much more than a placebo effect to any form of talk therapy,[130] which tend to take an exceptionally long time to work in any case. Even some psychoanalysts admit this. Anthony Storr, for instance, wrote in his essay "The Concept of Cure" that "the evidence that psychoanalysis cures anybody of anything is so shaky as to be practically non-existent."[131] And child psychiatrist Robert Coles notes:

---

[122] L. Luborsky et al., "The researcher's own therapy allegiances: a "wild card" in comparisons of treatment efficacy," *Clin. Psychol. Sci. Pract.* 6 (1999): 95–106; 10.1093/clipsy/6.1.95.
[123] I. A. Cristea, C. Gentili, P. Pietrini, and P. Cuijpers, "Sponsorship bias in the comparative efficacy of psychotherapy and pharmacotherapy for adult depression: meta-analysis," *British Journal of Psychiatry* 210.1 (2017): 16–23.
[124] A. Khan, J. Faucett, P. Lichtenberg, I. Kirsch, W. A. Brown, "A systematic review of comparative efficacy of treatments and controls for depression," *PLoS One* 7.7 (2012): e41778.
[125] P. Cuijpers et al., "The effects of psychotherapy for adult depression are overestimated: a meta-analysis of study quality and effect size," *Psychological Medicine* 40.2 (2010): 211–223.
[126] Paul Moloney, *The Therapy Industry: The Irresistible Rise of the Talking Cure, and Why It Doesn't Work* (London: Pluto Press, 2013), 33.
[127] D. L. Rosenhan, "On Being Sane in Insane Places," *Science* 179 (1973): 250–258.
[128] See https://www.nature.com/articles/d41586-019-03268-y. Accessed August 23, 2023.
[129] P. Cuijpers and I. A. Cristea, "What if a placebo effect explained all the activity of depression treatments?" *World Psychiatry* 14.3 (2015): 310–311.
[130] W. Epstein, *Psychotherapy as Religion: The Civil Divine in America* (Reno: University of Nevada Press, 2006).
[131] Quoted in E. M. Thornton, *The Freudian Fallacy: Freud and Cocaine* (London: Grafton Books, 1986), 16–17.

As for psychological recovery or "transformation," psychiatrists can spend long, intimate months, if not years, with patients and not know why at a particular moment a person is suddenly, it seems, "better." In retrospect, we come up with formulations, explanations: such and such was "interpreted." We are less likely to mention the many times we have offered similar "insights" to other patients, even to the same patient, all to no avail.[132]

Psychotherapy relies, as an interview method designed to soften mental distress, on confessional healing, which makes it closer to religious ritual than scientific practice. And "if you make a treatment long and expensive enough," argues Dalrymple so brilliantly, "people will always find that it did them at least some good, for otherwise they would have wasted their time and money, and would look foolish – even to themselves."[133]

The philosopher Edwin Erwin sees the field of psychotherapy as being in a state of scientific crisis,[134] while psychology professor William Epstein found the most cited publications on the effectiveness of talking therapy to stand on shaky methodological grounds (too small sample sizes, not enough effort expended to make sure that study participants were randomly assigned, variations in participant outcome were downplayed, over-reliance on patient self-report, and so on).[135] After reviewing the literature of the past 50 years, Epstein wrote in 2006 that "there has never been a scientifically credible study that attests to the effectiveness of any form of psychotherapy for any mental or emotional problem under any condition of treatment."[136] The reason it is so immensely popular in the West, and especially the United States, despite its ineffectiveness is that it reaffirms the cultural values of individualism and self-sufficiency. This ultimately makes psychotherapy a civil religion in Epstein's view: "metaphors that condemn the lack of self-restraint as sin, debase patients for their deficits, and justify the deprivation of needed care."[137]

But psychology may be even more attractive than religion, because as many religions claim if you do this and that, salvation awaits in the afterlife. But psychology says that if you do those things, you can get salvation here on earth, just by stripping away all baggage that the human condition brings with it; you can be

---

[132] Robert Coles, *The Mind's Fate: Ways of Seeing Psychiatry and Psychoanalysis* (Boston: Little, Brown & Co., 1975), 202.
[133] Theodore Dalrymple, *Admirable Evasions: How Psychology Undermines Morality* (New York: Encounter Books, 2015).
[134] E. Erwin, *Psychotherapy and Philosophy* (New York: Sage, 1997).
[135] W. Epstein, *The Illusion of Psychotherapy* (New York: Transaction Publishers, 1996); Epstein, *Psychotherapy as Religion*; W. Epstein, *Empowerment as Ceremony* (New York: Transaction Publishers, 2013).
[136] Epstein, *Psychotherapy as Religion*, 220.
[137] Epstein, *Psychotherapy as Religion*, 192.

completely at peace with yourself and the world outside. What a depiction of heaven on earth! And who wouldn't want that? But in the process, it creates worse human beings. One usually pays for therapy, and the goal is to not to be "cured" (psychotherapists and counsellors hardly use that term anymore), but to somehow come to peace with oneself. But this is likely to leave one with a sense of moral superiority, given all the work done on the self. This is, of course, important, as one doesn't want antisemites to become more accepting of themselves as such.

The mathematician Benoit Mandelbrot has shown that measurements are always relative, as they depend on subjective choices, including the unit of measurement.[138] This is a fact scientist should always keep in mind. Yet the argument that psychotherapy is unscientific is especially convincing, as psychotherapy is based on what one is able to express about one's inner life during the interview process with a therapist. But for most of us it is harder to capture our feelings in words than we think. The philosopher Daniel Haybron calls this "affective ignorance."[139] And how could we? If I score a "4" out of 10 on an anxiety scale, is this double of what somebody else feels who scores a "2"? Haybron also points to the important fact that this is hardly addressed in the literature. A scholar who does address it is Elaine Scarry, who convincingly argues in her book *The Body in Pain: The Making and Unmaking of the World*, that pain is inexpressible, as it destroys language.[140]

Yet, the question here is not whether mental suffering exists or not, or if it is created by society, but whether psychotherapy is the answer to these problems. I'm not a therapeutic nihilist. I just don't think – based on the evidence – that psychotherapy is a compelling answer to the problem. If psychology were the solution to our mental distress, after over a century since its incorporation into more and more aspects of our lives, shouldn't it have solved things by now? But are we less mentally disturbed? We certainly have less friends and social connections on average. And the chance to engage in deep conversations with another person is not as common as many of us may need, especially during times of so many social uncertainties. So it comes as no surprise that people are increasingly drawn to the idea of therapy. However, it strikes me as remarkably naïve to think that a therapist could possibly make a change in one's life without having control over the client's financial and physical context, employment, and environment. On the contrary there are many people who quit smoking, stop drinking, create

---

[138] Benoit Mandelbrot, "How Long Is the Coast of Britain? Statistical Self-Similarity and Fractal Dimensions," *Science* 156 (1967): 636–638, https://doi.org/10.1126%2Fscience.156.3775.636.

[139] D. M. Haybron, *The Pursuit of Unhappiness: The Elusive Psychology of Well-Being* (Oxford: Oxford University Press, 2008).

[140] Elaine Scarry, T*he Body in Pain: The Making and Unmaking of the World* (New York: Oxford University Press, 1985), 19–20.

loving relationships, raise happy children, lose weight, or overcome painful experiences, all without psychological intervention. Or how else did we survive as a human species before the invention of psychology? What can somehow help are sympathetic, intelligent, focused and preferably in-person interactions with somebody perceived as an optimistic authority figure in treating a given issue, not whatever psychological theory and training the therapist follows. In other words: social interaction and the placebo effect, not psychology.

An antisemite would hardly see the hate inside himself as a problem to be fixed by a therapist. But could he meet a psychologist in an attempt to gain more insight about himself and start taking responsibility for what he feels, thinks, and does in regard to Jews? I assume that most psychologists sincerely believe that what they do helps people, their clients and society at large, and that their work alleviates distress. And that they deserve their status in society as experts of human behavior. And that their judgement of it is better than those who have not attended their extensive (and most often expensive) training, internalized their ideology, and obtained their degrees. After all, we are often told that "mental illness is just like any other illness," which puts psychologists on a level with medical doctors and nurses. But despite the fact that certain psychotherapists may claim to have turned their clients around, I am not aware of a single case where such an internal makeover has objectively taken place.

But "As in the religious confessional, failure in therapy is seldom considered to be a failure of the method or philosophy itself (or even of the practitioner), but of the patient's unwillingness to be honest about themselves or to work hard enough upon the techniques," writes Paul Moloney in *The Therapy Industry*.[141] The theory and method applied are right, it is just that antisemites don't come into the office and work hard enough on themselves, according to psychological reasoning. And, of course, one needs to have "faith in the therapist/counsellor" to improve whatever the patient/client brings to the table. Faith, as in religious ritual, may even be used by psychologists themselves. In this context, one does not speak of "willpower" anymore (with a few exceptions).[142] Too close is its association with the Nazis. If not "faith," psychologists may speak of "motivation," "desire," "effort," "intentionality," and the like.[143] Seeing failure in therapy as the client's fault – as if they don't show enough discipline to access their inner strengths – is thus a common view within the discipline, and a heritage of a time one thought about people in such problematic terms.

---

[141] Moloney, *The Therapy Industry*, 74.
[142] R. F. Baumeister and J. Tierney, *Willpower: Why Self-Control is the Secret of Success* (London: Penguin, 2010).
[143] Moloney, *The Therapy Industry*, 74; C. Feltham, "Whatever Happened to Free Will and Willpower?" *Critical Thinking in Counselling and Psychotherapy* (London: Sage, 2010).

A Problematic History

The sense that psychology's nature as a science is in question is nothing new. This goes back at least to Freud and his "discovery" of the unconscious. Of course, humans do not always act upon the motivations they claim to have or believe themselves to have. This does matter, but one does not need psychology to understand the unconscious. It was not even a discovery by Freud or the other early psychoanalysts, but was common sense even at that time. It was to be found in literature from Shakespeare[144] to Goethe,[145] in religious texts from St. Thomas Aquinas[146] and the Indian Vedas,[147] in the work of mathematicians like Leibniz,[148] and the philosophies of Spinoza,[149] Rousseau,[150] Kant,[151] Hume,[152] Scho-

---

[144] For instance: "When we should submit ourselves to an unknown fear" (*All's Well*, II, iii, 6); or "My mind is troubled, like a fountain stirr'd; And I myself see not the bottom of it" (*Troilus and Cressida*, III, iii, 311).

[145] For example: "Mood is something unconscious and is based on sensuality" (*Maxims and Reflections*, No. 1005); Goethe also claimed that he wrote *The Sorrows of Young Werther* "practically unconsciously;" quoted in Richard Askay and Jensen Farquhaar, *Apprehending The Inaccessible: Freudian Psychoanalysis and Existential Phenomenology* (Evanston, IL: Northwestern University Press, 2006), 79.

[146] "I do not observe my soul apart from its acts. There are thus processes in the soul of which we are not immediately aware." Quoted in: L. L. Whyte, *The Unconscious Before Freud* (New York: St. Martin's Press, 1978), 80.

[147] See, for instance: C. N. Alexander, "Growth of Higher Stages of Consciousness: Maharishi's Vedic Psychology of Human Development," in C. N. Alexander and E. J. Langer (eds.), *Higher Stages of Human Development: Perspectives on Human Growth* (New York: Oxford University Press, 1990), 286–341.

[148] "Our clear concepts are like islands which arise above the ocean of obscure ones;" "[Yet] it is not easy to conceive that a thing can think and not be conscious that it thinks." Quoted in Whyte, *The Unconscious Before Freud*, 99.

[149] "Men regard themselves as free, since they are aware of their will and their desires, and do not even in a dream think of the causes which determine their desiring and willing, as they do not know them." Quoted in: Whyte, *The Unconscious Before Freud*, 92.

[150] "The sound of the waves and agitation of the water caught hold of my senses and drove all other agitation from my soul, plunged it into delicious reverie . . . without any effort to think." Quoted in Leo Damrosch, *Jean-Jacques Rousseau: Restless Genius* (New York: Houghton Mifflin, 2005), 399.

[151] P. Leland, "Unconscious Representations in Kant's Early Writings," *Kantian Review* 23.2 (2018): 257–284. doi:10.1017/S1369415418000055.

[152] "The experimental reasoning itself, which we process in common with beasts, and on which the whole conduct of life depends, is nothing but a species of instinct or mechanical power, that acts in us unknown to ourselves; and in its chief operations, is not directed by any such relations or comparisons of ideas, as are the proper objects of our intellectual faculties." David Hume, *En-

penhauer,¹⁵³ or Hegel,¹⁵⁴ all the way back to the ancient Greek physician Galen, who lived around the 1ˢᵗ and 2ⁿᵈ century CE.¹⁵⁵ Freud's version is closest to E. von Hartmann's then prominent *Philosophy of the Unconscious*, which was published in 1868, decades before his "discovery of the unconscious."

Freud, however, spoke about these topics with academic authority and wrote about them scholarly, at least in his English translations. The "death instinct," for instance, is a term Freud never used in German, where he speaks instead of a "drive/impulse towards death" (*Todestrieb*), which certainly sounds less fascinating as an idea as a human "instinct." So also does the invented term "id" indicate something new, while Freud simply talks about "the It" (*das Es*) in German. Or "the I" (*das Ich*), which becomes "ego" in English and indicates a kind of self-centeredness. In some way, Freud became "Freud" only in his English translation, which concealed the common sense and banality of much of his writing, and by doing so gave a more scholarly sound to his other rather absurd ideas. But Freud marketed his ideas quite well, so that they appeared as scientific discoveries even to many German-speakers, despite their common-sense nature, and often even illogicality, absurdity, and plagiarism. And while doing so he failed to observe the most obvious of threats before the German invasion of Austria in 1938, before which he saw his real enemy, the one he was afraid of, as being not the Nazis but the Catholic Church.¹⁵⁶ While for Rainer Maria Rilke, Freud was "uncongenial and in places hair-rising",¹⁵⁷ James Joyce called psychoanalysis "neither more nor less than blackmail".¹⁵⁸ Being asked about his take on Freud and Jung, his close friend

---

quiry Concerning Human Understanding: A Critical Edition (Oxford: Oxford University Press, 2006 (1776)), 81–82.
153 "If . . . certain events or circumstances become for the intellect completely suppressed . . . the gaps that thus arise are filled up at pleasure; thus madness appears. For the intellect has given up its nature to please the will: the man now imagines what does not exist. Yet the madness which has thus arisen is now the lethe of unendurable suffering; it was the last remedy of harassed nature, i.e., of the will." Arthur Schopenhauer, *The World as Will and Idea* (London: Ludgate Hill, 1886), 169.
154 "Manifestations of vitality on the part of individuals and peoples, in which they seek and satisfy their own purposes, are, at the same time, the means and instructions of a higher and broader purpose of which they know nothing – which they realize unconsciously." Quoted in Whyte, *The Unconscious Before Freud*, 140.
155 Whyte, *The Unconscious Before Freud*.
156 Dalrymple, *Admirable Evasions*.
157 Rainer Maria Rilke, "Letter to Lou Andreas-Salomé, 20. Jan. 1912," in *Rainer Maria Rilke and Lou Andreas-Salomé: The Correspondence*, ed. and translated by Edward Snow and Michael Winkler (New York: Norton, 2006), 184.
158 Quoted in: Richard Ellmann, *James Joyce* (Oxford: Oxford University Press, 1959), 538.

Maria Jolas replied that "it was a remarkable sign of his intelligence that he didn't fall for psychoanalysis when it was so current. He started beyond it."[159]

Much has been written about the grotesque nature of Freud's ideas.[160] A virginal patient of his was told that her cough was caused by her unconscious desire to perform oral sex on her father, for instance.[161] Even his own wife called psychoanalysis "a form of pornography."[162] Despite this, admirers like Stephen Frosh still speak of Freud's "discoveries"[163] while applying the Oedipus Complex with all its bizarreness to the issue of antisemitism.[164] Other scholars, like E. M. Thornton, thankfully point to Freud's severe cocaine addiction, which influenced his grotesque theories. Thornton describes how users of the drug often fall victim of a "peculiar messianic obsession. The addict is gripped by an exaggerated and pathological conviction that he alone has 'the truth' and that he has an urgent mission to communicate this truth to all mankind."[165] Psychologists after Freud, notwithstanding which school they belong to, often still speak with an authority otherwise uncommon in social sciences. I do not intend to deny some of the few valuable experiments conducted in psychology, such as Richard Nisbett's fascinating work on the *Geography of Thought*, or Elizabeth Loftus' work on false memory. Both are valuable works because they challenge common notions within psychology (more about them later on). But, argues Theodore Dalrymple,

> the overall effect of psychological thought on human culture and society, I contend, has been overwhelmingly negative because it gives the false impression of greatly increased human self-understanding where none has been achieved, it encourages the evasion of responsibility by turning subjects into objects where it supposedly takes account of or inter-

---

[159] Richard M. Kain, "An Interview with Carola Giedion-Weckler and Maria Jolas," *James Joyce Quarterly*, 11.2 (1974), 120.
[160] See for instance: Richard Webster, *Why Freud Was Wrong: Sin, Science and Psychoanalysis* (New York: Basic Books, 2005); Frederick Crews, *Freud: The Making of an Illusion* (New York: Metropolitan Books, 2017); Dalrymple, *Admirable Evasions*; Jeffrey Moussaieff Masson, *Against Therapy: Emotional Tyranny and the Myth of Psychological Healing* (New York: Athenaeum, 1988); Thornton, *The Freudian Fallacy*.
[161] Crews, *The Making of an Illusion*, 603.
[162] Crews, *The Making of an Illusion*, 418.
[163] Stephen Frosh, "Freud, Psychoanalysis and Anti-Semitism," *The Psychoanalytic Review* 91 (2004): 309.
[164] Stephen Frosh, *Hate and the "Jewish Science": Anti-Semitism, Nazism and Psychoanalysis* (New York: Palgrave Macmillan, 2005); Frosh calls himself a "sympathetic critic" who finds psychoanalysis to be "aggravating and infuriating, yet also exciting and enlightening — not just in turn, but all at the same time." See Stephen Frosh, *For And Against Psychoanalysis* (2nd ed.; New York: Routledge, 2006), xi.
[165] Thornton, *The Freudian Fallacy*, 13–14.

ests itself in subjective experience . . . It is ultimately sentimental and promotes the grossest self-pity, for it makes everyone (apart from scapegoats) victims of their own behavior.[166]

This is true, of course, only if one strips psychology to its core and takes valuable lessons away that are often branded as "psychological insight" even they are from other schools of thought like stoicism or religious studies. Viktor Frankl's *Man's Search for Meaning* is an example. Despite the extraordinary success of the book on the popular market, where it is seen as a source of moral guidance, it has, however, been criticised by several Holocaust scholars, as Frankl "voluntarily requested to perform unskilled lobotomy experiments approved by the Nazis on Jews."[167] He was hence booed and called a "nazi pig" while attempting to give a lecture at the Institute of Adult Jewish Studies in New York in 1978.[168] Authors such as Erwin Staub[169] and Robert Jay Lifton[170] have both written on psychology's active involvement in genocide. Lifton, himself a psychiatrist, also writes about the complicity of German doctors in the Holocaust. Hans Asperger, for instance, cooperated with the Nazis by evaluating the "usefulness level" of children and sending them to the Am Spiegelgrund "clinic" which, as he knew, took part in child euthanasia.[171] But of course, the case of Frankl is a more complex one, as he was also a Holocaust survivor.[172]

The Nazi slur certainly applies much more aptly to another correspondent of Freud. The founder of analytical psychology, Carl Gustav Jung, who later in life broke with him, was antisemitic. Ugly statements such as "the Aryan unconscious

---

166 Dalrymple, *Admirable Evasions*.
167 Craig Newnes, "Judaism and the psy project," in Craig Newnes (ed.), *Racism in Psychology: Challenging Theory, Practice and Institutions* (New York: Routledge, 2021), 103; See also: T. E. Pytell, "Redeeming the unredeemable: Auschwitz and man's search for meaning," *Holocaust and Genocide Studies* 17.1 (2003): 89–113.
168 Newnes, "Judaism and the psy project," 103; See also: Pytell, "Redeeming the unredeemable," 89–113.
169 E. Staub, *The Roots of Evil: The Origins of Genocide and Other Group Violence* (New York: Cambridge University Press, 1989).
170 R. J. Lifton, *The Nazi doctors: Medical killing and the psychology of genocide* (London: Little, Brown & Co., 1989).
171 H. Czech, "Hans Asperger, National Socialism, and "race hygiene" in Nazi-era Vienna," *Molecular Autism* 9.29 (2018): 29. https://doi.org/10.1186/s13229-018-0208-6; Edith Sheffer, *Asperger's Children: The Origins of Autism in Nazi Vienna* (New York: W.W. Norton & Co., 2018).
172 At the same time, there was also a horrific debate within the field in the United States on the question of whether "feebleminded" adults and children should be killed. See, for instance, H. Steven Moffic, "Is There a Cure for Anti-Semitism?" in H. Steven Moffic et al. (eds.), *Anti-Semitism and Psychiatry: Recognition, Prevention, and Interventions* (New York: Springer, 2020), 345.

has a greater potential than the Jewish unconscious"¹⁷³ are his. The sentence stems from a 1934 article of Jung entitled "The State of Psychotherapy Today":

> The Jews have this peculiarity in common with women; being physically weaker, they have to aim at the chinks in the armor of their adversary. The Jewish race as a whole—at least this is my experience—possesses an unconscious which can be compared with the Aryan only with reserve. Creative individuals apart, the average Jew is far too conscious and differentiated to go about pregnant with the tensions of unborn futures. The Aryan unconscious has a higher potential than the Jewish; that is both the advantage and the disadvantage of a youthfulness not yet fully weaned from barbarism. In my opinion it has been a grave error in medical psychology up till now to apply Jewish categories—which are not even binding on all Jews—indiscriminately to Germanic and Slavic Christendom. Because of this the most precious secret of the Germanic peoples—their creative and intuitive depth of soul—has been explained as a morass of banal infantilism, while my own warning voice has for decades been suspected of anti-Semitism. This suspicion emanated from Freud. He did not understand the Germanic psyche any more than did his Germanic followers [or better: "parrots"]. Has the formidable phenomenon of National Socialism, on which the whole world gazes with astonished eyes, taught them better? Where was that unparalleled tension and energy while as yet no National Socialism existed?¹⁷⁴ [brackets inserted for clarification]

This goes hand in hand with negative comments by Jung on the allegedly overmaterialistic values of psychology practised by Jews: "The differences which actually do exist between Germanic and Jewish psychology and which have long been known to every intelligent [or better "insightful"] person are no longer to be glossed over, and this can only be beneficial to science."¹⁷⁵ [brackets inserted for clarification]

Jung collaborated with the Nazis despite having been a Swiss national. After the Nazis ousted the Jewish chair and members of the German Medical Committee for Psychotherapy, M. H. Goering (cousin of one of the most prominent Nazi figureheads Hermann Goering) appointed Jung as its chair.¹⁷⁶ He accepted. Shortly after the Nazis took power, on June 21, 1933, he gave an interview with Radio Berlin, stating: "Only the self-development of the individual, which I consider to be 'the supreme goal of all psychological endeavour', can produce consciously responsible

---

173 Avner Falk, *Anti-Semitism: A History and Psychoanalysis of Contemporary Hatred* (Westport, CT: Praeger, 2008), 110–111.
174 Carl J. Jung, "Civilization in Transition," in Gerhard Adler, Michael Fordham, and Sir Herbert Read (eds.), *Collected Works of C. G. Jung: Volume 10* (2nd ed.; trans. R. F. C. Hull; Princeton: Princeton University Press, 1970), 157–173. Quoted in Masson *Against Therapy*.
175 Jung, "Civilization in Transition," 533.
176 Sharon Packer, "How Anti-Semitism and the Shoah Helped Shape Twentieth-Century Psychiatry," in H. Steven Moffic et al. (eds.), *Anti-Semitism and Psychiatry: Recognition, Prevention, and Interventions* (New York: Springer, 2020), 83.

spokesmen and leaders of the collective movement. As Hitler said recently, the leader must be able to be alone and must have the courage to go his own way."[177] And in 1938, he gave an interview with an American correspondent that was published in *Hearst's International-Cosmopolitan* in 1939, in which he demonstrated his admiration for Mussolini ("I couldn't help liking Mussolini"[178]), as well as Hitler:

> There is no question but that Hitler belongs in the category of the truly mystic medicine man. As somebody commented about him at the last Nürnberg party congress, since the time of Mohammed nothing like it has been seen in this world. This markedly mystic characteristic of Hitler's is what makes him do things which seem to us illogical, inexplicable, curious and unreasonable . . . So you see. Hitler is a medicine man, a form of a spiritual vessel, a demi-deity or, even better, a myth . . .[179]

Thomas Kirsch writes in *The Jungians: A Comparative and Historical Perspective* that "In today's world of psychotherapy, one cannot be a Jungian without having to answer the charge that Jung was both a Nazi and anti-Semitic."[180] And Daniel Burston points out in *Anti-Semitism and Analytical Psychology* that "Jungians must grapple candidly with the history of anti-Semitism *within* Analytical Psychology, and not just society at large."[181]

Jeffrey Moussaieff Masson goes even further by arguing that "Jung's psychotherapy contains attitudes that are compatible with his collaboration. With its coercion and disdain for the real traumas that people experience, there is a deep strain of fascism running through Jung's psychotherapy."[182] After all, Jung wrote about the contact between whites and blacks:

> In South Africa the Dutch, who were at the time of their colonizing a developed and civilized people, dropped to a much lower level because of their contact with the savage races. The savage inhabitants of a country have to be mastered. In the attempt to master, brutality rises in the master. He must be ruthless. He must sacrifice everything soft and fine for the sake of mastering savages. Their influence is very great; the more surely they are dominated, the more savage the master must become. The slave has the greatest influence of all, because he is kept close to the one who rules him.[183]

---

177 William McGuire and R. F. C. Hull, eds., *C.G. Jung Speaking: Interviews and Encounters* (Princeton: Princeton University Press, 1977), 59–66.
178 McGuire and Hull, *C.G. Jung Speaking*, 115–135.
179 McGuire and Hull, *C.G. Jung Speaking*, 115–135.
180 Thomas Kirsch, *The Jungians: A Comparative and Historical Perspective* (New York: Routledge, 2000), 132.
181 Daniel Burston, *Anti-Semitism and Analytical Psychology: Jung, Politics and Culture* (New York: Routledge, 2021), 4.
182 Masson, *Against Therapy*.
183 *New York Times* interview reprinted in McGuire and Hull, *C.G. Jung Speaking*, 12.

And a paper Jung read at a congress in the presence of Freud gives further evidence to the ugliness of his thoughts: "The causes for the [sexual] repression can be found in the specific American Complex, namely in the living together with lower races, especially with Negroes. Living together with barbaric races exerts a suggestive effect on the laboriously tamed instinct of the white race and tends to pull it down."[184]

It is sometimes hard to distinguish in the work of psychologists between their political views and their psychological observations. Erich Fromm provides a prominent example of the left. This, unfortunately, happens in other disciplines, too, such as politics, sociology, or economics. But the degree to which Jung's mysticism gets represented as scientific discoveries (while his antisemitism and racism are largely ignored) is unknown to other social sciences. Here Freud was right. It's simply "the work of a snob and a mystic."[185]

The scene regarding Freud's other fellows is often dark, too, and consists of much one would certainly not expect from self-proclaimed experts of human relations: denunciations, betrayal, envy, backbiting, excommunications (all quite similar to academic departments these days). Eventually, nine of the first Viennese psychoanalysts (about one in seventeen) committed suicide,[186] a proportion some 20 times the norm.[187] A possible reason could be that they were drawn to the field of psychoanalysis in the first place because they had trouble functioning as human beings. But one must also note that psychoanalysis did not seem to have helped them much. Freud (as so many people drawn to psychology) was a deeply troubled person,[188] and his absurd ideas are hard to see as anything other

---

[184] Quoted in Fredric Wertham, *A Sign for Cain: An Exploration of Human Violence* (London: Robert Hale, 1968), 91 and Masson, *Against Therapy*.
[185] Quoted in: John Beebe, "Understanding consciousness through the theory of psychological types," in Joseph Cambray and Linda Carter (eds.), *Analytical Psychology: Contemporary Perspectives in Jungian Analysis* (London: Routledge, 2004), 83.
[186] Dalrymple, *Admirable Evasions*.
[187] C. Feltham, *Counselling and Counselling Psychology: A Critical Examination* (Ross-on-Wye: PCCS Books, 2013), 27.
[188] Or in the words of Vladimir Nabokov: "The ordeal itself is much too silly and disgusting to be contemplated even as a joke. Freudism and all it has tainted with its grotesque implications and methods appears to me to be one of the vilest deceits practiced by people on themselves and on others. I reject it utterly, along with a few other medieval items still adored by the ignorant, the conventional, or the very sick." See: Vladimir Nabokov, "Interview with Alvin Toffler," *Strong Opinions* (London: Penguin, 1990), 20.

than a cry for help and a reflection of his drug abuse. Or, as the acclaimed writer Karl Kraus said at the time, "psychoanalysis is the disease it purports to cure."[189]

Ideas About Antisemitism

But what has stemmed from these troubled times regarding the understanding of the antisemitic mind? In 2020, H. Steven Moffic found the right words when he talked in *Anti-Semitism and Psychiatry: Recognition, Prevention, and Interventions* only about a "potential" to provide "ideas" about antisemitism.[190] But at other times Moffic seems to present common sense as scientific discoveries. In his contribution to the volume, "Is There a Cure for Anti-Semitism?," he writes something that to me exposes the superficiality of much of psychological research:

> Over time, a common assumption has been that there is a hidden conspiracy theory that the Jewish people are trying to take over the world. Recent research finds that such conspiracy theories increase when personal alienation or anxiety are combined with feelings that society is unstable.[191]

I believe there is not much illuminating in this common-sense observation, which gets presented as the result of scientific research. And Moffic makes rather obvious errors in his work on antisemitism: "Anti-semitism can arise even in regions where Jews are absent, as was the case in Japan during the 1820s and 1830s, when the Japanese expressed hostile views of Jews even though they had never met one."[192] This is, however, not possible, as Japan was cut off from the rest of the world until 1853.[193] In fact, antisemitism came to Japan through the Japanese version of *The Merchant of Venice*, one of the first foreign plays translated and pro-

---

189 Thomas Szasz, *Anti-Freud: Karl Kraus's Criticism of Psycho-analysis and Psychiatry* (Syracuse: Syracuse University Press, 1990).
190 "In the last century, the fields of psychiatry and psychology emerged, potentially to add new insights into anti-Semitism and how to reduce it. The remaining chapters in this edited volume convey the most cutting-edge psychological ideas on anti-Semitism," in H. Steven Moffic et al. (eds.), *Anti-Semitism and Psychiatry: Recognition, Prevention, and Interventions* (New York: Springer, 2020), 15.
191 Moffic, "Is There a Cure for Anti-Semitism," 344; the work he referred to is M. Moyer, "People drawn to conspiracy theories share a cluster of psychological features," *SciAm* 320.3 (2019): 58–63.
192 Moffic et al., *Anti-Semitism and Psychiatry*, 4.
193 https://www.britannica.com/biography/Matthew-C-Perry#ref1115075. Accessed August 23, 2023.

duced in Japan, and the *Protocols of the Elders of Zion*,[194] which became quite popular in Japan at the beginning of the 20th century, although it was evident that it was a forgery.[195]

But what are those "potential ideas" the field of psychology could provide us with? For one, there is Richard Morrock's grotesque understanding of antisemitism as a "defense mechanism against a variety of repressed feelings, most of them stemming from birth trauma. Although everyone is a survivor of the birth process, some births are more traumatic than others, and some birth traumas are reinforced by childhood."[196] But what is one supposed to take from this? If only women were better at giving birth there would be less people around killing Jews? Despite this utter nonsense, antisemites are not in need of psychological treatment for their trauma. Otherwise, the Nuremberg Trials would have been injustice. Antisemitism is not the fear of public speaking or hating spiders,[197] nor the fault of mothers giving birth in a traumatizing way. The scientist's job is not to help antisemites relieve their pain and suffering caused by their being antisemites, but to find ways to combat their crimes and lies.

Moreover, given what the field has produced, psychology suggests that antisemitism is not even a treatable condition, at least not by anything it can offer. The psychoanalytic literature on antisemitism is quite large.[198] A title search (conducted in August 2022) of the journals included in the Psychoanalytic Electronic Publishing (PEP) database for "antisemitism" or "anti-semitism" yields 86 original papers. The references of these papers point to hundreds of other contributions which are not included in the PEP database. A comprehensive review of the entire psychoanalytic literature about antisemitism would extend beyond the scope of this book. The following contributions, however, demonstrate larger trends within the field that in part border on esotericism.

---

194 David G. Goodman, "The Protocols of the Elders of Zion in Japan," in Esther Webman (ed.), *The Global Impact of The Protocols of the Elders of Zion: A Century-old Myth* (New York: Routledge, 2011), 161–174.
195 Christopher L. Schilling, *The Japanese Talmud: Antisemitism in East Asia* (London: Hurst, 2023).
196 Richard Morrock, "'The Ancient Enemy': The Psychology of Anti-Semitism The Journal of Psychohistory," *New York* 40.2 (2012): 103–114.
197 This sentence is inspired by a brilliant Jewbelong.com slogan posted on Instagram on December 23, 2021: "Feel free to hate spiders, and public speaking. But give us a break already. Signed, The Jews." https://www.instagram.com/p/CX05G1WsN6J/?utm_medium=copy_link. Accessed August 23, 2023.
198 Andrew (Nachum) Klafter, "Anti-Semitism: A Psychoanalytic Perspective," in H. Steven Moffic et al. (eds.), *Anti-Semitism and Psychiatry: Recognition, Prevention, and Interventions* (New York: Springer, 2020), 169.

While antisemitism is not the main theme of Freud's *Moses and Monotheism*, it does deal with the subject. Circumcisions could cause "castration anxiety" among gentiles, goes the argument.[199] And Christian Jew-hate is seen as a form of collective sibling rivalry and jealousy towards the "older brother" Judaism,[200] while Jews adapted for their survival certain characteristics such as stubbornness.[201] Unsurprisingly, *Moses and Monotheism* has received much criticism due to parts of it being provocative,[202] implausible (antisemitism in Muslim societies despite circumcisions), uncomfortable,[203] or painfully absurd.[204] Hence, very few scholars give *Moses and Monotheism* serious consideration these days. One of them is Jewish studies scholar Steven Weitzman of the University of Pennsylvania, who is sceptical but who still finds the book "strangely compelling" because of Freud's "perfect correspondence between the internal realm of the unconscious and the external realm of history."[205] An observation that seems to be no more than psychobabble. Consequently, Weitzman's *The Origins of the Jews* appears at times more Freudian fanfiction than scholarship. Nevertheless, Freud's ideas could persuade other established scholars to buy into his nonsense, too. The psychiatrist and neuroscientist Mortimer Ostow saw castration anxiety as one of the reasons for antisemitism, as well. He also understood antisemitism as a way to displace suicidal impulses.[206] But following this odd idea, would Jews be needed to help antisemitic individuals stay alive instead of killing themselves?

There is also a tendency toward uncomfortable victim blaming in some of the psychological literature on antisemitism. C. G. Schoenfeld sees Jewish behavior as provoking antisemitism by its religious rituals, which can trigger resentment among non-Jews by conveying a message of superiority.[207] For his argument he

---

199 Sigmund Freud, "Moses and Monotheism: three essays," in James Strachey (ed.), *The standard edition of the complete psychological works of Sigmund Freud, Volume XXIII (1937–1939): Moses and Monotheism, an outline of psychoanalysis and other works* (London: Hogarth Press, 1964), 87–92.
200 Freud, "Moses and Monotheism," 91.
201 Freud, "Moses and Monotheism," 105–106.
202 Klafter, "Anti-Semitism," 171.
203 V. E. Morpurco, "Why does Moses and Monotheism still make us uneasy? Freud, psychoanalysisanti-Semitism," *The Italian Psychoanal Annual* 1 (2007): 203–220.
204 R. Williams, "Freudian psychology," in A. Richardson and J. Bowden (eds.), *A New Dictionary of Christian Theology* (London: SCM Press, 1983), 220.
205 Steven Weitzman, *The Origins of the Jews: The Quest for Roots in a Rootless Age* (Princeton: Princeton University Press, 2017), 183.
206 Mortimer Ostow, *Myth and Madness. The Psychodynamics of Antisemitism* (New York: Transaction Publishers, 1996), 91.
207 C. G. Schoenfeld, "Psychoanalysis and anti-Semitism," *Psychoanalytic Review* 53.1 (1966): 24–37.

cites Ernest Jones' smear of a Jewish "superiority complex in respect to brain power."[208] This kind of theorizing seems to me not only wrong but controversial, to say the least. Interestingly, the Ontario Human Rights Commission gives as an example in their "Policy on preventing discrimination based on creed" paper: "A psychologist speaks about the 'Jewish personality' and explains contemporary social behaviour based on presumed and attributed psychological characteristics allegedly shared by all Jewish people."[209]

Even though Jean-Paul Sartre was a philosopher, not a psychologist, he offered a psychoanalytic theory in *Anti-Semite and Jew*. In his understanding, antisemitism is a primitive passion in which the antisemite exists in a mental state where (s)he is willing to believe what (s)he knows on some level to be untrue, because it is emotionally attractive to believe in such falsehood. Political or economic problems can then be blamed on Jews. Therefore, "it is the anti-Semite who makes the Jew."[210] In other words, the only content of the definition of a Jew is given by non-Jewish others. But Jews are capable of providing content to the idea of themselves, just like any other group. Further, there are obviously variations in Jewish identity through history and place, which makes Sartre's view on antisemitism unconvincing.

Lajos Székely describes the analytic treatment of antisemitic patients and concludes from them that antisemitism is a mystical belief in secret societies and magical powers, which results from infantile fantasies.[211] Unfortunately, the argument is as simple as it is unconvincing. Many of us engage in some form of infantile superstitions, be it horoscopes, fortune tellers, haunted places, making a wish after blowing out candles, or coin tossing. But not all of us obsess over Jews controlling the world with magical powers.

Stanley Rosenman locates the problem in childhood as well, reasoning that antisemitism would stem from brutal, abusive parenting.[212] But, of course, this can't explain the phenomenon, as not all people with abusive parents become antisemites. Moreover, it is entirely unconvincing that all antisemites had brutal parents.

---

208 E. Jones, "The psychology of the Jewish question," in *Essays in applied psychoanalysis*, Vol. 1 (London: Hogarth, 1951).
209 https://www.ohrc.on.ca/en/policy-preventing-discrimination-based-creed/3-background. Accessed August 23, 2023.
210 Jean-Paul Sartre, *Anti-Semite and Jew: An Exploration of the Etiology of Hate* (New York: Schocken, 1976 (1948)), 49.
211 Lajos Székely, "Tradition and infantile fantasy in the shape of modern antisemitism," *Scandinavian Psychoanalytical Review*, 11.2 (1988): 160–177.
212 Stanley Rosenman, "A critique of classical psychoanalytic theories of anti-Semitism: a commentary on M. Ostrow's myth and madness: the psychodynamics of anti-Semitism," *The American Journal of Psychoanalysis* 58.4 (1998): 417–433.

Antisemites come in various forms, rich and poor, Western, Middle Eastern, men, women, young, old, smart, and stupid. It is certainly tempting to point to one simple trait that psychology could uncover, one which all antisemites share, such as brutal parents or a neglectful childhood. But Rosenman's idea neglects the complexity of human life and morality. We don't suffer when we are young and are then excused for the rest of our lives as survivors of childhood.

Similarly, Jean-Claude Stoloff believes that it "is during early childhood that biases, such as antagonism toward Jews, are formed,"[213] without giving scientific proof to what can only be described as an assumption, most likely a bad one. Given the spread of the problem across geography, religion, culture, gender, age, and so on, it seems a good guess to point to childhood as the one thing all antisemites have in common: they were all children once. But it is unconvincing to suggest that people can't adapt antisemitism later on in life, but that the root of the problem must be found in one's childhood. After all, more and more research shows that we have generally overemphasised the role of childhood development. We now know of the plasticity of the brain,[214] and that personality traits continue to change even in adulthood.[215] Stoloff's argument seems out of touch with the findings regarding human development from the last two decades at least.

In his contribution to *Anti-Semitism and Psychiatry Recognition, Prevention, and Interventions*, Andrew (Nachum) Klafter asks himself if "psychoanalytic theories offer any insight into the question of why Jews have so frequently been the object of fascination, hatred, and persecution throughout world history." Despite his belief in psychoanalysis in general, his answer is thoughtful:

> Anti-Semitism became a fact of Western culture, but not a fact of the human mind. Psychoanalysis helps us understand the dark, violent urges inside human beings that are expressed openly when social conditions allow it. These conditions include civil wars, violent revolutions, and apocalyptic religious movements, which have led to horrific episodes of anti-Semitism, among other forms of racial persecution. But how and why these conditions come about is a question of history, not psychoanalysis.[216]

---

213 Jean-Claude Stoloff, "Understanding the Current Resurgence of Anti-Semitism: The Situation in France," in H. Steven Moffic et al. (eds.), *Anti-Semitism and Psychiatry: Recognition, Prevention, and Interventions* (New York: Springer, 2020), 277.
214 Of course, there is also a rather confused public discourse around the term "neuroplasticity" that often gets over-evangelized.
215 See for instance Ravenna Helson, Virginia S.Y Kwan, Oliver P. John, and Constance Jones, "The growing evidence for personality change in adulthood: Findings from research with personality inventories," *Journal of Research in Personality* 36.4 (2002): 287–306.
216 Klafter, "Anti-Semitism," 176.

But unfortunately, when it comes to collective violence and antisemitism, Klafter falls back on Milgram. This is surprising, as Klafter writes in 2020, after scholars like Gina Perry have – as described – shown how Milgram had manipulated his research results.[217]

Theodore Isaac Ruben, who has served as president of the American Institute for Psychoanalysis, argues in *Anti-Semitism: A Disease of the Mind* that the antisemite secretly wishes to become a Jew. This idea is quite confusing, as he also classifies Jewish self-hate as a form of antisemitism.[218] But if this is the case, are self-hating Jews just secretly wishing to be Jewish?

And of course, antisemitism is not a "disease" or, as it is sometimes described, a "disease of men,"[219] "herpes virus,"[220] or "epidemic."[221] "I would call it an intellectual disease," wrote historian Paul Johnson, "a disease of the mind, extremely infectious and massively destructive. It is a disease to which both human individuals and entire human societies are prone."[222] Comparing it to a disease at first makes a great deal of sense, as it opens up a discussion about infections, toxicity, mutability, and contagion. But it is, nevertheless, too weak of a description, even as a metaphor. It does not help to explain the rise of antisemitic political movements,[223] and does not fully grasp the difficulty of getting rid of it since "there is no comparable effort to finding a cure,"[224] as Ruth Wisse observes. "Those infected with the disease have no strong incentive to seek a cure since they do not suffer the physical consequences; and contrarily, the Jewish victims, who are understandably eager to diagnose the illness and discover a cure, have no access to the carriers and cannot heal those who consider themselves heathy."[225]

---

[217] Gina Perry, *Behind the Shock Machine: the untold story of the notorious Milgram psychology experiments* (New York: The New Press, 2012). See also: Gina Perry et al., "Credibility and Incredulity in Milgram's Obedience Experiments: A Reanalysis of an Unpublished Test," *Social Psychology Quarterly* 83.1 (2019) 88–106.
[218] Theodore Isaac Ruben, *Anti-Semitism: A Disease of the Mind – A Psychiatrist Explores the Psychodynamics of a Symbol Sickness* (New York: Continuum, 1990).
[219] Delphine Horvilleur, *Anti-Semitism Revisited* (London: MacLehose Press, 2021), 85.
[220] "Understanding Antisemitism – Deborah Lipstadt." https://www.youtube.com/watch?v=IXo0-hX4kmk. Accessed August 23, 2023.
[221] See for instance: https://jcpa.org/stopping-the-viral-epidemic-of-anti-semitism-in-the-united-states/. Accessed August 23, 2023.
[222] Paul Johnson, "The Anti-Semitic Disease," *Commentary* (June 2005).
[223] Steven Beller, *Antisemitism: A Very Short Introduction* (Oxford: Oxford University Press, 2007), 2–3.
[224] Ruth Wisse, "The Anti-Semite's Pointed Finger," *Commentary* (November 2010): 24, 27.
[225] Ruth Wisse, "Holocaust, or War Against the Jews?" in Michael Brown (ed.), *Approaches to Antisemitism: Context and Curriculum* (New York: The American Jewish Committee, 1994), 24.

Antisemitism characterized as a disease has also been criticised for being a mirror image of the antisemitic comparison of Jews with disease.[226] And, more crucially, it undermines individual responsibility. This is highly important. If an action is a symptom of a disease, it is treated differently. Sneezing in front of somebody is morally and legally different from spitting on someone. Or, as psychiatrist Thomas Szasz puts it: "We moderns do not believe in punishing disease or patients for having disease. We do not imprison, much less kill, mentally ill persons; we excuse them of their crimes and hospitalize them . . . If anti-Semitism is a disease, then the Nazi leaders were very sick indeed, and the Nuremberg trials were one of the great injustices of the 20th century."[227] But of course, this was not the case. Kenneth L. Marcus argues that "the disease metaphor is problematic for the reason that makes it comforting, that is, because it implies that anti-Semitism is wholly foreign to healthy persons in the post-Holocaust West."[228] Empirical research has demonstrated that antisemitism can be found in otherwise healthy humans.[229] And "there was no evidence that those convicted at the Nuremberg war crimes trials suffered from 'psychosexual' pathologies any more than other people did, or that their childhood experiences were particularly aberrant,"[230] writes Dawes. "Nor did they appear to be particularly 'bloodthirsty' people; they all claimed that they had simply been doing their jobs – even when it meant exterminating people,"[231] something Hannah Arendt famously termed the "banality of evil."

Marcus is right when he argues that "by defining the anti-Semite as an extreme, foreign, virulent other, we create a myth of our own healthy bodies as untouched by this disavowed condition."[232] Describing antisemitism as a disease, mental disease, or epidemic is, therefore, not helpful.[233] Antisemitism is not something one catches like a disease. The mind gets trapped in it, like a disaster, a self-inflicted disaster. And it is one psychology can't help with.

---

[226] Kenneth L. Marcus, "Accusation in a Mirror," *Loyola University Chicago Law Journal* 43 (2012): 357–393.
[227] Thomas Szasz, Letter to the Editor, *Commentary* (October 2005) quoted in Kenneth L. Marcus, *The Definition of Anti-Semitism* (Oxford: Oxford University Press, 2015), 49.
[228] Marcus, *The Definition of Anti-Semitism*, 49.
[229] Marcus, *The Definition of Anti-Semitism*, 50.
[230] Robyn M. Dawes, *House of Cards: Psychology and Psychotherapy Built on Myth* (New York: The Free Press, 1996), 200–201.
[231] Dawes, *House of Cards*, 201.
[232] Marcus, *The Definition of Anti-Semitism*, 50.
[233] Nor is it particularly helpful as a metaphor in other contexts. At times it even reaches forms of intellectual nonsense. Three-time Pulitzer Prize winner Thomas Friedman, for instance, called 9/11 a "geopolitical pandemic," the 2008 financial crisis a "financial pandemic," and climate change an "atmospheric pandemic." See https://www.youtube.com/watch?v=gBa7wPPBGAo. Accessed August 23, 2023.

Pharma

Rubin, who came via psychoanalytic interpretation to the conclusion that antisemitism is a form of psychopathology, argued with the concept of "symbol sickness" that antisemites project self-hate onto Jews and even suggested medication as a potential solution.[234] *Anti-Semitism: A Disease of Mind* was published over thirty years ago, and I'm not aware of any such drug having been invented that could cure an antisemite ever since.[235]

A reason that "antisemitism as illness" has not been widely adopted is due to the lack of a market for any kind of drug or treatment; mental illnesses are invented as a category, not discovered. The British psychiatrist David Healy has demonstrated well how diagnostic fashions in psychiatry accompany marketing strategies.[236] Depression was not very common in psychiatric hospitals in the United Kingdom in the 1950s. Nor was there a specific antidepressant on the market. "When the antidepressant action of certain compounds was first proposed," writes the counselling psychologist Paul Moloney,

> drug companies were initially reluctant to develop and launch such products. In an unconscious alliance of interests, influential psychiatrists expanded and popularised the view of depression as a common biologically based disorder, amenable to chemical treatment and as yet frequently unrecognised. This concept had the dual benefit of vastly expanding both the market for psychiatric drugs and the operations of psychiatry beyond the asylum. From the 1980s, the research and promotional activities of drug companies transformed everyday "bad nerves" to "anxiety" and then into "depression" in order to create a wider market for their new SSRI antidepressants, including the brand Prozac.[237]

This took place as profits from minor tranquillisers went down, not because of new scientific discoveries, goes the argument.[238] In the decade after Prozac was introduced to the market, the number of people treated for depression tripled.[239]

---

234 Rubin, *Anti-Semitism*.
235 My scepticism includes psychedelics that are often naively evangelized as a cure for societal problems, including antisemitism. See: Christopher L. Schilling, "The Case Against Psychedelic Judaism" in *Zen Judaism: The Case Against a Contemporary American Phenomenon*, Palgrave Macmillan, Cham: 2021; See also: https://forward.com/opinion/554342/mdma-shows-promise-for-healing-ptsd-and-political-extremism/ (access date August 18, 2023).
236 D. Healy, *Pharmageddon* (Berkeley: University of California Press, 2012).
237 Moloney, *The Therapy Industry*, 38.
238 D. Healy, "Shaping Discontent: The Roles of Science and Marketing," in P. Pietikainen (ed.), *Modernity and Its Discontents: Sceptical Essays on the Psychomedical Management of Malaise* (Stockholm: Axel and Margaret Johnson Foundation, 2004).
239 Paul Moloney, *The Therapy Industry*, 39.

Carl Elliott, professor at the Center for Bioethics at the University of Minnesota, notes in this regard:

> A pharmaceutical public relations strategy . . . is to sell a treatment by selling a disease. To sell Prilosec, you have to sell acid reflux; to sell Lotronex, you have to sell irritable bowel syndrome; to sell Viagra, you have to sell erectile dysfunction; to sell Adderall, you have to sell ADHD. You market a treatment by convincing doctors and patients to diagnose the illness that your drug or procedure treats.[240]

It is a well-known yet unresolved problem that pharmaceutical companies are not (primarily) acting in the interest of the ill but in the pursuit of profit. In fact, they are among the most profitable industries around the world.[241] The corruption of parts of academia is a result of pharmaceutical companies incentivising scholars to claim what they might otherwise not, commission papers that end up in peer-reviewed journals – thereby manipulating doctor's opinions – and suppress studies that show those compounds are little more than sugar pills in their effectiveness to treat a condition.[242] Recent research has thrown serious doubt on the claim that chemical imbalance causes mental illness at all,[243] which should not surprise anyone. If not discussed publicly as much as it should have been, it was known among many scientists for decades.[244] The scientific evidence even points to the contrary, with some scientists worrying that medicated people suffering from depression are more likely to remain symptomatic over the long run.[245] Or did we really believe we would be able to design our personalities with SSRIs?

---

240 Carl Elliott, "Pharmaceutical Propaganda," in Jonathan M. Metzl and Anna Kirkland (eds.), *Against Health: How Health Became the New Morality* (New York: New York University Press, 2010), 96.
241 Healy, *Pharmageddon*.
242 Moloney, *The Therapy Industry*, 39; Healy, *Pharmageddon*.
243 J. Moncrieff, R. E. Cooper, T. Stockmann et al., "The serotonin theory of depression: a systematic umbrella review of the evidence," *Mol Psychiatry* (2022). https://doi.org/10.1038/s41380-022-01661-0; Anne Harrington, *Mind Fixers: Psychiatry's Troubled Search for the Biology of Mental Illness* (New York: W.W. Norton & Co., 2019).
244 See for instance Michael A. Posternak et al., "The Naturalist Course of Unipolar Major Depression in the Absence of Somatic Therapy," *The Journal of Nervous and Mental Disease* 194.5 (2006) or H. E. Pigott, A. M. Leventhal, G. S. Alter, and J. J. Boren, "Efficacy and Effectiveness of Antidepressants: Current Status of Research," *Psychother Psychosom* 79 (2010): 267–279. Doi: 10.1159/000318293.
245 Rif S. El-Mallakh, Yonglin Gao, and R. Jeannie Roberts, "Tardive dysphoria: The role of long term antidepressant use in-inducing chronic depression," *Medical Hypotheses* 76 (2011): 769–773; Giovanni A. Fava, "Holding On: Depression, Sensitization by Antidepressant Drugs, and Prodigal

When the 5th edition of the Diagnostic and Statistical Manual of Mental Disorders (DSM-5) started to require from its clinician-authors disclosure of financial ties to pharmaceutical companies, over half of them admitted "significant industry interests."[246] Despite the horrors of the Opioid Crisis, "big pharma" operates as it does because it is a business that relies on a medical need that can be associated with a compound over which the company has intellectual property rights. And as companies seek to increase their profits, what pharma does apart from its useful research is, often, manufacture a disease (depression in Japan, for instance)[247] or broaden its definition so that it applies to more customers in larger quantities.

And herein lies a danger, which could produce more antisemitism. Mental illnesses are not at all stable categories. They change with the economic and social climate and what constitutes "healthy" or "normal." When sadness and loneliness became taboo in Western societies, it opened the door for "depression." And, of course, the interest of patients and lawyers in seeking compensation plays a role in it. After all, it seems easier to claim compensation for an individual who has been diagnosed with PTSD than for someone who is simply anxious. "Yet the clinical and research evidence suggests that most of the disorders itemised in the DSM are best seen, not as organic brain illnesses, but as how most of us would respond to prolonged or intense loneliness, despair, deprivation, or mistreatment," writes Moloney.[248]

The psychologist Nick Haslam coined the term "concept creep" to describe a trend when psychological concepts of harm and pathology "expanded their meanings so that they now encompass a much broader range of phenomena than before" and consequently run "the risk of pathologizing everyday experience".[249] "Indeed, a general trend toward the medicalization of virtually every emotional and cognitive state is upon us,"[250] fears English professor and disability researcher at the

---

Experts," *Psychother Psychosom* 64 (1995): 57–61; Irving Kirsch, *The Emperor's New Drugs: Exploding the Antidepressant Myth* (New York: Basic Books, 2011).
246 M. Angell, "The Illusions of Psychiatry," *New York Review of Books* (14 July 2011); http://www.nybooks.com/articles/archives/2011/jul/14/illusions-of-psychiatry/?pagination=false&printpage=true. Accessed August 23, 2023.
247 Ethan Watters, *Crazy Like Us: The Globalization of the American Psyche* (New York: The Free Press, 2010).
248 Moloney, *The Therapy Industry*, 49.
249 Nick Haslam, "Concept Creep: Psychology's Expanding Concepts of Harm and Pathology," *Psychological Inquiry* 27.1 (2016), 1; see also Frank Furedi, "The Cultural Underpinning of Concept Creep," *Psychological Inquiry*, 27.1 (2016), 34–39.
250 Lennard J. Davis, "Obsession: Against Mental Health," in Jonathan M. Metzl and Anna Kirkland (eds.), *Against Health: How Health Became the New Morality* (New York: New York University Press, 2010), 127; see also H. Gilbert Welch, Lisa Schwartz, and Steven Woloshin, "What's

University of Illinois at Chicago, Lennard J. Davis. While normal human behavior gets increasingly labelled a mental problem, Jewish religious observance has already been described by some mental health workers as "obsessive-compulsive disorder" or "eating disorder." This is something Kate Miriam Loewenthal and Barry Marcus investigated in their important research.[251] Of course, every case might be unique, as it is unclear what comes first: Is psychology being used by antisemites to deny Jews their religious and cultural identity, or does the field lead to the development of such antisemitic ideas? In a market in which academics are incentivised to invent and expand categories for drugs, it could easily lead to normal Jewish religious behavior being labelled as behavior worthy of modification by means of pharmaceuticals. And this is clearly antisemitic. The practise of Judaism is not a mental health issue. But neither is a child who "often talks excessively," "often fidgets" or "squirms," "often leaves seat," or "often runs about." Yet, these are classified as symptoms of ADHD by the DSM-5,[252] instead of characteristics of a normal child (who is probably bored in class, perhaps due to bad teaching, is facing overcrowded classrooms, or is energetic due to too much sugar for breakfast). But somehow a market for the drugs must be found and definitions of ADHD expanded, even if this targets the most vulnerable, most normal human beings. After all, psychoactive drugs have been advertised for other absurdities before. An advertisement in the *Archives of General Psychiatry* talked in 1970, for instance, about an unmarried "psychoneurotic" lesbian in need of Valium to find a man,[253] while an advertisement in the *American Journal of Psychiatry* in 1965 suggested taming feminist women with the drug.[254]

In the end, antisemitism is simply not a phenomenon clinical psychology could reasonably address. But it is a phenomenon that clinical psychology could exacerbate and fuel.

Making Us Sick Is an Epidemic of Diagnoses," *New York Times* (2 January 2007); http://www.nytimes.com/2007/01/02/health/02essa.html. Accessed August 23, 2023.

251 Kate Miriam Loewenthal and Barry Marcus, "Jewish Stereotypes in Psychiatric Diagnosis and Treatment," in H. Steven Moffic et al. (eds.), *Anti-Semitism and Psychiatry: Recognition, Prevention, and Interventions* (New York: Springer, 2020), 185–192.

252 https://www.wsj.com/articles/do-psychologists-cause-mental-illness-11621548927. Accessed August 23, 2023.

253 Quoted in Jonathan M. Metzl, *Prozac on the Couch: Prescribing Gender in the Era of Wonder Drugs* (Durham, NC: Duke University Press, 2003), 6–7.

254 Valium add in *American Journal of Psychiatry* 121 (1965): xii–xiii, quoted in Metzl, *Prozac on the Couch*, 16.

Chapter III
The Way the World Goes Mad, and a "WEIRD" Understanding of it

While judging psychology, it must be clarified that different countries have different "traditions" and histories of the phenomenon. While France and French-speaking regions largely cherish psychoanalysis, behaviouralism is stronger in Anglo-Saxon countries. Israel is – as so often – somewhere in the middle.[255] Consequently its (ab)uses have been different, too. Yet, a general and unfortunate trend can be identified, in which psychological categories are being exported from the West to non-Western countries and consequently cause mental disturbances in those parts of the world. The global spread of ideas is, without a doubt, a good thing. And preventing knowledge from circulating can cause obvious harm. The fact that during Communism many ground-breaking and truly innovative Western concepts were outright banned in the Soviet Block (such as approaches to autism spectrum disorders) speaks to this.[256] But expanding a problem globally before introducing a "cure" for it is something the field of psychology is quite capable of as well.

Creating Mental Health Issues

The French philosopher La Rochefoucauld went so far as to say: "There are some people who would never have fallen in love, if they had not heard there was such a thing."[257] Whether this is true or not, if an issue is labelled as the "discovery of truth" or a "scientific finding," such a label can certainly cause its spread. Jerome K. Jerome jokes in *Three Men in a Boat* that one can persuade oneself into the

---

[255] I'm thankful to one of the anonymous reviewers for reminding me of this distinction.

[256] I'm thankful to one of the anonymous reviewers for pointing me to this fact. In this context, it is also worth mentioning that pioneering research on autism spectrum disorders by the Soviet scientist Grunya Efimovna Sukhareva were surprisingly not credited by the Austrian Hans Asperger, most likely for the reason that she had a Jewish background. See Edith Sheffer, *Asperger's Children: The Origins of Autism in Nazi Vienna* (New York: W.W. Norton & Co., 2018); D. A. Sher and J. L. Gibson, "Pioneering, prodigious and perspicacious: Grunya Efimovna Sukhareva's life and contribution to conceptualising autism and schizophrenia," *Eur Child Adolesc Psychiatry* 32.3 (2021): 475–490. https://doi.org/10.1007/s00787-021-01875-7.

[257] Quoted in: https://www.theschooloflife.com/article/the-great-philosophers-la-rochefoucauld/. Accessed August 23, 2023.

symptoms of a hundred illnesses simply by reading a medical textbook. These days, we are no longer unhappy (which often leads to bad decisions), but rather we "suffer from depression"; we are not worried about unstable employment, but "suffer from chronic anxiety"; and we don't have anxious moments anymore, but experience "PTSD" as a condition requiring decades of drugs and therapy. In the current version of the DSM, a diagnosis of depression requires simply a "depressed mood" or a "loss of interest or pleasure" together with three of the following symptoms:

(3) Significant weight loss when not dieting or weight gain, or decrease or increase in appetite nearly every day;
(4) A slowing down of thought and a reduction of physical movement (observable by others, not merely subjective feelings of restlessness or being slowed down);
(5) Fatigue or loss of energy nearly every day;
(6) Feelings of worthlessness or excessive or inappropriate guilt nearly every day;
(7) Diminished ability to think or concentrate, or indecisiveness, nearly every day;
(8) Recurrent thoughts of death, recurrent suicidal ideation without a specific plan, or a suicide attempt or a specific plan for committing suicide.[258]

Well, I guess we are all mad, aren't we? And potentially less responsible. Until a few decades ago, however, people did not generally identify with mental illness. Dean Schuyler, head of the depression section at the National Institute of Mental Health (NIMH), advised Americans in the 70s that depression was episodic and experiences of it "will run their course and terminate with virtually complete recovery without specific intervention."[259] Yet, this wise understanding of mental suffering could not withstand the therapeutical wave that was unfolding in Western culture. Already back in the 1950s, one of the leading American critics of the 20th century, Lionel Trilling, remarked that the ideas of psychoanalysis were becoming the "slang of our culture."[260] And more and more conversations in Western societies become oddly clinical these days, with couples quoting their therapists back at each other in arguments and 18-year-old college students speaking of their "history of depression." Or when the hardship in one's life and the expected aspects of the human condition lead to the "experience of mental health issues," or when exhausted and mistreated workers are incentivised to take a "mental health day." Or when poor New Yorkers fighting in cramped apartments have therapists trained in

---

[258] https://www.psycom.net/depression-definition-dsm-5-diagnostic-criteria/. Accessed August 23, 2023.
[259] Quoted in: https://unherd.com/2022/10/the-truth-about-depression-drugs/. Accessed August 23, 2023.
[260] Lionel Trilling, *Freud and the Crisis of Our Culture* (Boston: Beacon Press, 1955), 12.

conflict resolution helping them cope, instead of the city spending that money on alleviating the overcrowding.[261]

The human experience becomes increasingly medicalised when one is no longer "sad," "angry," or "lonely" but overrun by "mental illness." When a mental health charity in the UK commissioned a statue of Winston Churchill in a straitjacket,[262] they reduced a historical person to the category of "the depressed." As if Churchill wasn't a human being with flaws and achievements that we can judge and celebrate, but a manifestation of an illness. Nor does this reflect the self-image of a man who, in his first statement as British prime minister, stated: "I have nothing to offer but blood, toil, tears and sweat."[263]

In this view of the human condition, any activity becomes a question of psychological survival should well-being and comfort be temporarily absent. Police officers are seen as survivors of PTSD, or "CopShock";[264] therapists develop "compassion fatigue" by talking to their clients;[265] and housework, according to researchers at the University of Glasgow, makes people depressed: "the more housework you do, the more depression you report."[266] It is a culture that encourages one to regard personal problems and normal discomfort as part of some medical condition to which one may fall victim. Experiencing romance gets articulated in this medicalized slang as "catching feelings," while the promiscuous cannot help it: they are "sex addicts."

I do recognize that a lot of people, perhaps especially younger ones, suffer mentally these days. And perhaps much more so than in previous times. ("Perhaps," of course, because we do not and cannot know how previous generations have felt in comparison.) Yet labelling these problems as mental illnesses often leads to social isolation. After all, what could people tell someone who is medically categorized as "depressed" or "suffering from anxiety," as those are medical conditions that need to be treated by a professional? Yet, when someone tells of "sadness," this often leads to conversations and human support. Other humans might not be *the* solution to the complexity of the human mind and its malfunctions, yet it is hard to imagine *a* solution without human support. But there is a

---

[261] Eva S. Moskowitz, *In Therapy We Trust: America's Obsession with Self-Fulfillment* (Baltimore: The Johns Hopkins University Press, 2001), 4.

[262] http://news.bbc.co.uk/2/hi/uk_news/4795832.stm. Accessed August 23, 2023. To the best of my knowledge, this is an accurate summary of the charity's acts regarding the statue and a personal impression of the result of it.

[263] Quoted in https://www.cfr.org/blog/twe-remembers-churchills-blood-toil-tears-and-sweat. Accessed August 23, 2023.

[264] Allen R. Kates, *CopShock, Surviving Posttraumatic Stress Disorder (PTSD)* (Cortaro, AZ: Holbrook Street Press, 1999).

[265] Moskowitz, *In Therapy We Trust*, 5.

[266] http://news.bbc.co.uk/2/hi/health/2287960.stm. Accessed August 23, 2023.

general trend in Western societies to classify human suffering in medical categories and to isolate people mentally within asylums. This rather dehumanizing slang creates more loneliness and people who, left alone, feel more and more like medical categories, not responsible humans. This is especially true as people are increasingly incentivised to discover their mental illnesses on days such as the National Depression Screening Day or the National Anxiety Disorder Day.[267]

The lack of social engagement around individual mental suffering may also explain the extreme phenomenon of "mad pride,"[268] whose adherents celebrate their histories of mental illness. This is by no means representative of all people who suffer mentally, yet it is puzzling that some people cross this line between being open about mental struggles and fetishizing it. I would not think that such experiences would be anything to celebrate, to wish on a loved one, or to be proud of. One may argue that "mad pride" is justified inasmuch as it seeks to end the stigma surrounding mental illness and help people "come out." But this argument does not seem to me to hold much weight, as it divides society into the mad and the sane, hence causing further division. Freddie DeBoer writes for *Unherd* that the "combination of self-pity and self-aggrandisement is emblematic of our contemporary understanding of mental health" and tells of a thriving TikTok community of people who are proud to be autistic or who find their ADHD an adorable character trait.[269] But if one can celebrate suffering from depression or schizophrenia, it is conceivable that one could be led to celebrate the disorder of hating Jews, too. And who could blame antisemites, if they have no agency and aren't responsible for whatever terrible thing comes into their minds? "Were we wiser and more serious," DeBoer argues, "we might be able to see psychiatric disorders as both natural and lamentable, as beyond the control of the individual but still within their responsibility."[270]

But we so often aren't. In 2020, Paul Appelbaum, a professor of psychiatry at Columbia University, told in a *Forward* article about the spike of antisemitic violence in New York City, and articulated what seems to me an unspeakable error concerning who is a vulnerable victim and who a perpetrator: "There are people, some of whom have a mental illness, who are vulnerable to influence by the trends that are occurring around them in society. In a context in which anti-

---

[267] See for instance: https://news.vanderbilt.edu/2022/10/04/national-depression-screening-day-is-oct-6/. Accessed August 23, 2023.
[268] https://blog.oup.com/2019/06/mad-pride-end-mental-illness/. Accessed August 23, 2023.
[269] https://unherd.com/2022/04/mental-illness-doesnt-make-you-special/. Accessed August 23, 2023.
[270] https://unherd.com/2022/04/mental-illness-doesnt-make-you-special/. Accessed August 23, 2023.

Semitic rhetoric is prevalent, they will pick that up."[271] With statements like this, are we just a step away from antisemitism itself becoming yet another mental disorder that psychologists "discover," and thereby expand their professional authority to wherever this moral and social conflict may be found?

In 1952 the American Psychiatric Association listed homosexuality in their Diagnostic and Statistical Manual of Mental Disorder (DSM) as a mental disorder. This scandalous mistake was only revoked in 1973. Attraction to the same sex has since been freed from the burden of being seen as a mental illness by the profession in the United States, at least according to its DSM. But what happens if the profession stumbles into the mistake of classifying something bad, such as antisemitism, as a mental disorder, even if only until the scientific community changes its mind? The message to the general public would have terrible consequences: "antisemitism is no longer a mental disorder" would be the headline. A society that puts everything into psychological categories, from unhappiness, shyness, and gambling to smoking or overeating, until the absurdity of it becomes too apparent, risks causing much harm. The inflation of psychiatric categories is detrimental, both in relation to entirely normal aspects such as same-sex attraction and in cases of hatred based on race, ethnicity, or religion.

Considering the wide media coverage of psychological "findings" about human nature, one must worry about how many people might convince themselves that they can't help but be antisemitic because of some birth trauma, in-group bias, gene, brain scan, or personality type. What someone might take from psychological ideas is an "it's my mind, I can't help myself; I have these anxieties, so I can only surrender to being an antisemite." People often use psychology to evade responsibility for their thoughts and actions, which makes the field problematic, as it intends to promote exactly the opposite.

This can be seen with the spread of eating disorders, for example, which seem to spread as the public becomes increasingly aware of their existence. This can be seen with the so called "Werther effect," named after an increase of suicides among young men after the publication of Goethe's *The Sorrows of Young Werther*, in which the lovesick hero kills himself. Similarly, there have been increases in "copycat suicides" following media reports on the topic, especially involving celebrities. And this can be seen with the spread of mental fragility due to the tort system, which often rewards suffering. In cases where plaintiffs have an interest in maximizing the psychological harm they have suffered, which is of course difficult to disprove and easy to fake. But, "the person who fakes neurosis

---

271 https://forward.com/news/438117/mental-illness-anti-semitic-hate-crimes-crown-heights-homelessness/. Accessed August 23, 2023.

for long enough actually becomes neurotic,"[272] writes prison physician and psychiatrist Anthony Malcolm Daniels under his penname, Theodore Dalrymple. "If you claim not to be able to concentrate or to leave the house, eventually your concentration will be destroyed or you will become housebound. Since most people do not like to think of themselves as frauds, the symptoms continue even after the case is settled."[273] The same can be true about undisprovable physical symptoms after injury should they show no evidence of physical pathology, as Andrew Malleson tells it so brilliantly in his book *Whiplash and Other Useful Illnesses*.[274] Dalrymple does not claim that horrible events may not have psychological consequences, but claims that "the real cause of much psychological disability, then, is the tort system, without which sufferers might be psychologically much more robust."[275] The phenomenon of antisemitism must, therefore, be prevented from becoming a psychological category and evading human responsibility as those who endorse this evil way of thinking are not victims.

An Americanization of Mental Health

An amplification of this problem is the Americanization of the world's understanding of the human mind and the concomitant spread of mental illnesses, be it eating disorders in Hong Kong, depression in Japan, or PTSD in Sri Lanka. The problem has been well documented by Ethan Watters in *Crazy Like Us – The Globalization of the American Psyche:*

> Over the past thirty years, we Americans have been industriously exporting our ideas about mental illness. Our definitions and treatments have become the international standards. Although this has often been done with the best of intentions, we've failed to foresee the full impact of these efforts. It turns out that how a people in a culture think about mental illnesses – how they categorize and prioritize the symptoms, attempt to heal them, and set expectations for their course and outcome – influences the diseases themselves. In teaching the rest of the world to think like us, we have been, for better and worse, homogenizing the way the world goes mad.[276]

---

272 Theodore Dalrymple, *Admirable Evasions: How Psychology Undermines Morality* (New York: Encounter Books, 2015).
273 Dalrymple, *Admirable Evasions*.
274 Andrew Malleson, *Whiplash and Other Useful Illnesses* (Montreal: McGill-Queen's University Press, 2005).
275 Dalrymple, *Admirable Evasions*.
276 Ethan Watters, *Crazy Like Us: The Globalization of the American Psyche* (New York: The Free Press, 2010), 2.

What is especially problematic, according to Watters, is that "indigenous forms of mental illness and healing are being bulldozed by disease categories and treatments made in the USA."[277] But if antisemitism becomes a psychological category, determined by mostly American psychologists, this further eliminates the possibility of local, indigenous ways to treat the problem. I'm concerned with the possibility of antisemitism being exported as a "disease," just as the Japanese have been made "depressed" by American pharma companies in the way that it became a culturally acceptable category to feel sad. "I suffer from prejudice towards Jews" may become an unwanted eventuality, if antisemitism is described and categorized as disease or mental illness in a world where many Americans industriously export such ideas. And this is not that unlikely given the fact that the field of psychology needs ever more categories to support the ever-growing group of mental help professionals. Psychotherapy training has even been described as a "pyramid selling scheme" by the psychotherapist Nick Totton. "Far more practitioners are being trained than there are clients available for them."[278] And "The only way to get enough therapy and counselling paid for . . . is to get the state and other institutions to pay for it. For this to happen, psychotherapy and counselling must present themselves as somehow *medical*" [italics in original].[279] It is not farfetched to imagine a call for Western-trained psychologists to rush into whatever part of the world in which antisemitism (or genocide) is on the rise to deliver "psychological first aid" to the broken minds there that need to be healed of anxiety or aggression. But as we can't even manage to treat antisemitism effectively in the West, why would their approach bring any benefit to completely different cultural settings?

This is a general problem: Western – especially American – understandings of mental illnesses are mapped on the entire world and indigenous concepts of mental illness that do not fit are classified in the American diagnostic manual (DSM-IV, pages 845–849) as something exotic sounding, like "Culture-Bound Syndromes." As if Western medical knowledge is always the truth and others mistaken. But "the experience of mental illness cannot be separated from culture,"[280] writes Watters. "We can become psychologically unhinged for many reasons . . . Whatever the cause, we invariably rely on cultural beliefs and stories to understand what is happening. Those stories, whether they tell of spirit possession or

---

277 Watters, *Crazy Like Us*, 3.
278 Nick Totton, "'The baby and the bathwater': 'professionalisation' in psychotherapy and counselling," *British Journal of Guidance and Counselling* 27.3 (1999): 315.
279 Totton, "'The baby and the bathwater,'" 316.
280 Watters, *Crazy Like Us*, 5–6.

serotonin depletion, shape the experience of the illness in surprisingly dramatic and often counterintuitive ways."[281]

When psychologists claim that antisemitism stems from XY, this can be a dangerous thing, as the lesson for people in those countries could be that it is only natural for them to think and feel and act the way they do in regard to Jews. After all, it's their birth trauma or anxiety issue. Social Sciences should not commit the same injustice as certain drug companies do when they sell the very disease that must exist for their drug to (purportedly) cure. A psychological category of "antisemitism" is not only unscientific, but potentially dangerous; it would negate society, history, economics, and personal responsibility in its very making.

It is concerning to see the loss of diversity in our different perceptions of mental illness and its treatments. And are we sure Western academics have all the answers? A writer for *CNN* and the *The Washington Post* even feared a "pogrom in the Upper West Side of Manhattan"[282] in the summer of 2021. Fortunately, it has not come to this, but this is at least something that has moved closer to the realm of possibility with antisemitic left and right-wing demagogues in American politics and public life. Shifting public perceptions of Jews in America should be a wakeup call, as should the increase of public violence, online antisemitism, and a poorly performing police force. If antisemitism is now a life-threatening problem to Jews even in places like Manhattan and Pittsburgh, doesn't that tell us that Americans have not come to a solution to the problem any more than others around the globe?

"WEIRD" People

My book *The Japanese Talmud* explores antisemitism in East Asia, a region of the world with almost no Jews or Jewish history. Yet East Asia shows some of the world's highest rates of it. This can manifest in disturbing ways: a concentration camp themed restaurant in Taiwan, or a "Adolf Hitler Techno Bar & Cocktail Show" in South Korea. But at the same time, various books with "Talmud" in the title have become bestsellers and are found in vending machines and public schools, while private "Jewish education" institutions have opened across South Korea and claim to improve children's IQ. People can stay at a "Talmud Business Hotel" in Taiwan, while there is a legend in Japan of its people being a Lost Tribe of Israel. Other cases are at first hard to put into Western categories. Thus did "Anne's day" (named after Anne Frank) become a euphemism for menstruation in Japan.

---

[281] Watters, *Crazy Like Us*, 6.
[282] https://twitter.com/thatpeterfox/status/1395562472774545409. Accessed August 23, 2023.

The image of Jews in East Asia is often a strange mixture of opposites, a paradoxical blend of admiration and mocking, identification and denial. And even though there are almost no Jews who could fall victim to direct antisemitism in the region, the topic is nevertheless important, as it demonstrates how we have misunderstood the problem as a global phenomenon, just as psychologists have for a long time completely misunderstood the diversity of global thinking. This makes the work of Joseph Henrich and what he termed "WEIRD" people so immensely important.[283] He demonstrates that academic psychology does not teach us about *the* human mind, as humans think quite differently across different cultures. And as I argue, the mind of an antisemite may differ not in degree of hate at different places across the globe, but in kind.

In 2010, a remarkable article by Henrich et al. in *Behavioral and Brain Science* addressed the largely overlooked global diversity of thinking and Western bias when it comes to psychological test subjects, who are normally "western, educated, industrialised, rich and democratic," or "WEIRD" for short. In fact, most subjects of psychological experiments are U.S. American undergraduate students making some extra money or getting course credit by participating in studies on their campus.[284] Thus, psychological research designed to produce knowledge about human behaviour and thought processes "may have instead uncovered truths about a thin slice of our species—people who live in . . . (WEIRD) nations."[285] This is important, because humans are fundamentally cultural animals, so cultural differences inform our different norms, attitudes, even our the perceptions of things like color.[286] But, unfortunately, the scientific literature still remains largely WEIRD,[287] and does not adequately address the issue of different

---

[283] Joseph Henrich, *The WEIRDest People in the World: How the West Became Psychologically Peculiar and Particularly Prosperous* (New York: Farrar, Straus & Giroux, 2020).
[284] J. Henrich, S. J. Heine, and A. Norenzayan, "The weirdest people in the world?" *Behavioral and Brain Sciences* 33.2–3 (2010): 61–83.
[285] M. Muthukrishna, A. H. Bell, J. Henrich et al., "Beyond Western, Educated, Industrial, Rich, and Democratic (WEIRD) Psychology: Measuring and Mapping Scales of Cultural and Psychological Distance," *Psychological Science* 31.6 (2020): 678–701; see also Henrich, Heine, and Norenzayan, "The weirdest people in the world?".
[286] M. Gelfand, *Rule Makers, Rule Breakers: Tight and Loose Cultures and the Secret Signals that Direct our Lives* (New York: Scribner, 2019); R. Boyd, *A Different Kind of Animal: How Culture Transformed Our Species* (Princeton: Princeton University Press, 2017).
[287] M. S. Rad, A. J. Martingano, and J. Ginges, "Toward a psychology of *Homo sapiens*: Making psychological science more representative of the human population," *Proceedings of the National Academy of Sciences* 115 (2018): 11401–11405.

perceptions across the globe, nor the differences within WEIRD countries.[288] The psychological study of antisemitism is no exception. Its research is fundamentally on WEIRD antisemites, not on the rest of the world.[289]

Richard Nisbett is a social psychologist at the University of Michigan. His book *The Geography of Thought: How Asians and Westerners Think Differently . . . and Why* informs our understanding of East/West cognitive differences. His groundbreaking research shows how Westerners (primarily Europeans, Americans, and citizens of the British Commonwealth) and East Asians (principally Chinese, Koreans, and Japanese people) have kept very different systems of thought for thousands of years. Western thought rests on the assumption that the nature of objects can be grasped in terms of straightforward rules and formal logic by putting them into categories that define what rules to apply to the object in question. East Asians, on the other hand, tend to understand objects as part of their contexts.

A reason psychology is so successful in the West – in comparison to East Asia – is that it emphasises the individual over the situation when it comes up with categories like "the depressed" or identifies an individual with low self-esteem. However, in a mind that has developed in East Asia, a person always exists within a setting. Anthropologist Edward T. Hall argues in *Beyond Culture* that the idea that there can be attributes that are not conditioned on social circumstances is foreign to the Asian mind.[290] To Westerners it makes sense to see a person as having characteristics that are independent of circumstances, and of moving from setting to setting without changing fundamentally. In the East Asian mind, however, one's being tends to be somewhat fluid and conditional. Philosopher Donald Munro, for instance, talks of East Asians understanding themselves "in terms of their relation to the whole, such as the family, society, Tao Principle, or Pure Consciousness."[291] Self-descriptions of the Western-trained mind are produced very much out-of-context (the depressed, the psychopath, and so on), while Eastern minds tend to think in terms of context: "I'm thoughtful at work" or "I'm funny with my friends." A study found that Japanese, for instance, find it very difficult to describe themselves without pointing out a particular kind of situa-

---

[288] Henrich, Heine, and Norenzayan, "The weirdest people in the world?"; R. R. McCrae, A. Terracciano, and 79 Members of the Personality Profiles of Cultures Project, "Personality profiles of cultures: Aggregate personality traits," *Journal of Personality and Social Psychology* 89 (2005): 407–425; Muthukrishna, Bell, Henrich et al., "Beyond Western, Educated, Industrial, Rich, and Democratic (WEIRD) Psychology."
[289] Christopher L. Schilling, *The Japanese Talmud: Antisemitism in East Asia* (London: Hurst, 2023).
[290] Edward T. Hall, *Beyond Culture* (New York: Anchor Books, 1976).
[291] Donald Munro, "Introduction," in *Individualism and Holism: Studies in Confucian and Taoist Values* (Ann Arbor: University of Michigan Press, 1985), 1–34.

tion: at work, with friends, at home, and so on.[292] Westerners, on the other hand, might find it hard to describe themselves in the context of a situation. The Western belief that "I am what I am" becomes in East Asia more of an "I'm Ichiro's friend." Academic psychology thus makes sense coming from a Western point of view; and its "discoveries" concerning the antisemitic mind are, if valid at all, only about a small, WEIRD part of the world.

It would be a great mistake to leave East Asia out when thinking of antisemitism. Cases of what I term "Buddhist antisemitism,"[293] seen in thinkers such as D. T. Suzuki and Hakuun Yasutani, are likely to be left undetected if studies do not develop a more global outlook.[294] Or the antisemitic nature of the terrorist attack by the Buddhist *Aum Shinrikyo* cult on Tokyo's subway, which killed 13 and seriously injured 54 other commuters.[295] Or antisemitic cults like the Korean Unification Church of Sun Myung Moon (whose followers are referred to as "Moonies" by some people). The Unification Church proclaimed that Jews had lost their status as the chosen people since the new Messiah, Sun Myung Moon, was born in Korea.[296] Moon himself has also made some terrible statements about the Holocaust, including that its Jewish victims were paying indemnity for the crucifixion of Jesus.[297] Especially since these Asian cults can have global outreach, they should be studied by antisemitism scholars. But this is admittedly a difficult task, as much of the literature on cults is based on the unverifiable findings of social psychology and is also ultimately quite "WEIRD."

---

[292] S. D. Cousins, "Culture and self-perception in Japan and the United States," *Journal of Personality and Social Psychology* 56 (1989): 124–131; see also M. H. Kuhn and T. S. McPartland, "An empirical investigation of self-attitude," *American Sociological Review* 19 (1954): 68–76.

[293] Christopher L. Schilling, "Buddhist Anti-Semitism," *Jewish Political Studies Review* 31.3–4 (22 February 2021). https://jcpa.org/article/buddhist-anti-semitism/. Accessed August 23, 2023.

[294] Schilling, "Why East Asia Matters to the Understanding of Antisemitism," *Journal of Contemporary Antisemitism* 6.2 (Fall Issue 2023); "On Symbolic Philosemitism in Japan," *Journal of Modern Jewish Studies* 19.3 (2020): 297–313; "The Problem of Romanticizing Israel-Taiwan Relations," *Israel Affairs* 24.3 (2018): 460–466; "Japanese Studies in Israel – A Response to Meron Medzini's 'From Alienation to Partnership: Israel-Japan Relation' in the *Contemporary Review of the Middle East*," *Japan Studies Review* XXIII (2019);.

[295] Schilling, "Buddhist Anti-Semitism."

[296] A. James Rudin, "A View of the Unification Church," *American Jewish Committee Archives* (1978). See also Schilling, *The Japanese Talmud*; and Christopher L. Schilling, "Jewish Seoul: An Analysis of Philo- and Antisemitism in South Korea," *Modern Judaism – A Journal of Jewish Ideas and Experience* 38.2 (2018): 183–197; https://doi.org/10.1093/mj/kjy002.

[297] Shoshanah Feher, "Maintaining the Faith: The Jewish Anti-Cult and Counter-Missionary Movement," in Anson D. Shupe and David G. Bromley (eds.), *Anti-Cult Movements in Cross-Cultural Perspective* (New York: Garland, 1994), 42.

Chapter IV
Psychohistory

Critics are right when they speak of a "contemporary obsession with (auto)biographies" that reflects a "culture of individualisation,"[298] especially in North America. The psychologist Svend Brinkmann rightfully believes "that there is something about the linear progression of the biography, in which events happen in chronological order, that has a reassuring effect in an accelerating culture that otherwise seems to be running amok."[299] It is certainly problematic that (auto)biographies celebrate the individual as the most important aspect of human history at the expense of social, economic, cultural, political, or demographic circumstances. An individual's journey to develop, struggle, change, and reflect is often thrilling to read, I must admit. But apart from the joy biographies can bring to the reader, they constitute a scholarly problem.[300] The sociologist Pierre Bourdieu spoke in this regard of the "biographical illusion" and a "socially irreproachable artifact."[301] Others describe the biography format as a "quixotic enterprise," due to the elusiveness of a historical actor's character,[302] or the impossibility of reconstructing from records the life of a person.[303] After all, we struggle to reconstruct even our own lives based on our memories. Stanley Fish made a point when he attacked modern biography in the *New York Times* as "Minutiae without Meaning" that comes up with "little more than a collection of random incidents, and the only truth being told is the truth of contingency, of events succeeding one another in a universe of accident and chance."[304]

---

[298] Svend Brinkmann, *Stand Firm: Resisting the Self-Improvement Craze* (New York: Polity, 2017), 86.
[299] Brinkmann, *Stand Firm*, 86.
[300] Christopher L. Schilling, "Review of Derek Penslar, *Theodor Herzl: The Charismatic Leader* (Jewish Lives)," *Jewish Political Studies Review* 31.3–4 (16 February 2021).
[301] Pierre Bourdieu, "The Biographical Illusion," in Paul du Gay, Jessica Evans, and Peter Redman (eds.), *Identity: A Reader* (Los Angeles: Sage, 2000), 297–303, at 301.
[302] Peter France and William St. Clair, "Introduction," in Peter France and William St. Clair (eds.), *Mapping Lives: The Uses of Biography* (Oxford: Oxford University Press, 2000), 2.
[303] William St. Clair, "The Biographer as Archaeologist," in Peter France and William St. Clair (eds.), *Mapping Lives: The Uses of Biography* (Oxford: Oxford University Press, 2000), 219–234; Leonard Cassuto, "The Silhouette and the Secret Self: Theorizing Biography in Our Times," *American Quarterly* 58 (2006): 1249–1261, at 1253–1254.
[304] Stanley Fish, "Just Published: Minutiae without Meaning," *New York Times* (7 September 1999): A19.

https://doi.org/10.1515/9783111349572-006

Often, biographies appear weirdly sexualized. Recent examples of this within Jewish studies include Derek Penslar's rather vulgar biographies of Theodor Herzl, in which "Zionism became a means by which he could expose his genitals."[305] At the same time, Penslar, a faculty member at Harvard,[306] portrays the homosexual Herzl – against all logic, evidence, historical context, and much of the existing literature on the topic – as a paedophile in his *Jewish Lives* biography with Yale University Press.[307] Such irresponsible exercises of theory validation and false understandings

---

305 Derek Penslar, "Zionism as Theodor Herzl's Life Project," in Nina Caputo and Mitchell B. Hart, (eds.), *On the Word of a Jew: Religion, Reliability, and the Dynamics of Trust* (Bloomington: Indiana University Press, 2019), 287.

306 Derek Penslar holds various positions at Harvard including director of the Center for Jewish Studies and director of undergraduate studies within Harvard's history department. He is a scholar of colonialism, postcolonialism, and Zionism, yet I am not aware of any scholarship of his on antisemitism. But he signed the Jerusalem Declaration on Antisemitism for which he has received criticism. In the words of Richard Landes, Penslar accepts even "'intemperate' language from critics of Israel as legitimate" while he does not "consider calls for the dissolution of Israel 'in and of themselves' antisemitic". Moreover, he does not see the BDS movement as antisemitic. See: https://fathom journal.org/a-remarkably-aggressive-naivete-a-response-to-derek-penslar-and-michael-walzer/ (Access date October 26, 2023); https://fathomjournal.org/why-i-signed-the-jda-a-response-to-cary-nelson-2/ (Access date October 26, 2023). The events at Harvard after the October 7, 2023 attack on Israel, including over thirty student groups and the celebration of genocide were disturbing and deeply concerning to me, to say the very least. Even if one takes into account that Harvard ranks top for campus antisemitism, they were a new low. See: https://www.thejc.com/news/news/report-says-harvard-university-ranks-top-for-campus-antisemitism-7PvcDHrjXKLseQC9zwHwf (Access date October 18, 2023); Oddly they got excused as a case of free speech by Harvard President Claudine Gay. The sudden invocation of free speech came as a surprise since Harvard ranked as America's worst college for free speech. See: https://rankings.thefire.org/rank (Access date October 18, 2023); I would hope for the horror of these events at his own university to lead Penslar to a re-evaluation of his disturbingly naïve understanding of antisemitism. A rethinking seems to be currently taking place among other signatories of the Declaration. In response to my question about whether the events on American campuses in October 2023 have led him to question his decision to sign the Jerusalem Declaration, Michael Walzer told me that he "thought, maybe wrongly, that the Jerusalem statement at least opened the way for argument and education." See: https://docs.google.com/document/d/e/2PACX-1vRrU_R4lJMubYBFX5KePu9RclIerKeXVWtEFKHvsetG7sXUTFdDfLF9TBJDe_Qra2Pmf1gM byfdrJdJ/pub (As of access date October 25, 2023 Penslar's name was missing as confirmed to me by an organizer). Unfortunately, this book went into print shortly after the events and can't comment on this further. See, however a very interesting and important article by Harvard PhD student J.J. Kimche: https://www.wsj.com/articles/harvard-shrugs-at-jew-hatred-hamas-attack-israel-civilian-murder-torture-rape-68f53256?page=1 (Access date: October 18, 2023).

307 Derek Penslar, *Theodor Herzl: The Charismatic Leader* (New Haven: Yale University Press, 2020), 31; see also Christopher L. Schilling, "The Strange Absence of LGBTQ Actors in the Historical and Political Writings of Derek J. Penslar," *Harvard Kennedy School LGBTQ Policy Journal* (19 June 2020); Schilling, "Review of Derek Penslar, *Theodor Herzl*"; and Christopher L. Schilling, "Review of Nina Caputo and Mitchell B. Hart, eds., *On the Word of a Jew: Religion, Reliability, and*

of historical circumstances and cultural differences can only fail to pass the test of genuine scholarship. The biography almost seems to have the objective of destroying Herzl's reputation rather than generating knowledge, or to portray a Jewish hero as a role model to his readers. This is very much in line with a general trend in biographies these days that view heroic figures as dysfunctional people and their achievements as driven by inner wounds rather than admirable character traits. *Theodor Herzl* says probably more about the cultural climate in which Penslar writes than it could ever say about the founder of Zionism. And superficial statements that could describe numerous individuals are presented by Penslar as academic insight: "[Herzl was in] an ongoing struggle to find meaning in life and to win recognition, which was the only way he could allay chronic and powerful depression,"[308] or "Herzl was psychologically exoskeletal, constructed from the outside in."[309]

Similarly, Saul Friedländer wrote a *Jewish Lives* biography in which he speculates that Franz Kafka may have been a paedophile in his thought-life: "What he alluded to, we do not know. Perhaps he opaquely refers to his sexual attraction to adolescents, even children? But these, like his homoerotic urges more generally, remained in the domain of fantasy. Could he have felt 'dirty' because of fantasies?"[310] It is beyond my understanding how this extremely serious, but entirely speculative, accusation adds anything to the production of knowledge. Especially

---

the Dynamics of Trust," *Jewish Political Studies Review* 31.3–4 (14 January 2020). Regarding Herzl's homosexuality, see for instance Ernst Pawel, *The Labyrinth of Exile: A Life of Theodor Herzl* (New York: Farrar, Straus & Giroux, 2011). In Penslar's description of Herzl, he avoids the term "paedophile" itself but writes: "Yet the marriage to Julie quickly soured, and after that, Herzl never found (or, apparently, sought) sexual satisfaction with individuals of either gender." See Penslar, "Zionism as Theodor Herzl's Life Project," 280; "he gave up on erotic love, marital or otherwise, and contented himself with fantasies of virginal and unattainable girls." On p. 286 Penslar further calls Heinrich Kana a "platonic friend" of Herzl, despite a vast amount of literature showing that Kana and Herzl were deeply in love with one another. On p. 280 he says: "Five months later, this desire to maintain contact with the object of his affections assumed the form of an obsession when, at a children's ball in Budapest, Herzl spied Magda Herz, Madeleine's niece, who he had held in his arms as a toddler and who was now thirteen (Herzl was twenty-six.) . . . Herzl grew fiercely jealous of boys who danced with her – so much so that 'I went out of my head completely. I had to force myself not to tell her, as to an adult, that I love her.' Herzl dreamed of her. In the following days he sought her out, finding her at an outdoor ice-skating rink and gazing at her from afar. Five days later he went back to the rink and did not find her . . . Herzl resolved to marry her, to wait the three years until she was of age . . . But then he began to doubt that his beloved's unique, ethereal charm would survive the transition to sexual maturity." See Penslar, *Theodor Herzl*, 31.
308 Penslar, "Zionism," 279.
309 Penslar, "Zionism," 290.
310 Saul Friedländer, *Franz Kafka: The Poet of Shame and Guilt* (New Haven: Yale University Press, 2013), 8.

since Friedländer attests that Kafka did not act upon it. Not to speak of his terrible style of writing. The passage reads to me as if the author meant paedophilia as a subcategory of homosexuality, which could not possibly have been his intention and would obviously be wrong.

Other biographies can slip into a melodramatic style. Jay Howard Geller's *The Scholems* is a recent example ("he is primarily excited about [. . .] exploring the strange new world that is America").[311] Geller has published widely on Freud's Jewish identity (*On Freud's Jewish Body* being such an unfortunate example) and has been member of the "Critical Theories of Antisemitism Network," an online group devoted to the exploration of antisemitism through psychoanalysis and Marxism among other approaches.[312] But while Geller ambitiously asks the readers of *The Scholems* "to re-approach the history of the Jews in Germany,"[313] he follows essentially a nationalist fabrication when he writes of a common German history before 1871, or else simply confuses Germany with Prussia. And he would do well to treat the fate of Holocaust victims such as Werner Scholem – of whom he writes, "He is already familiar with the world of the concentration camps, having been imprisoned since April 1933"[314] — with more dignity.[315] The Network went defunct in 2019.[316]

While historical biographies aren't scientific in nature, they aren't traditionally Jewish either. Yosef Hayim Yerushalmi showed in his influential book *Zakhor: Jewish History and Jewish Memory* that modern historiography is a concept foreign to traditional Jewish culture and that its growth coincided with a "decay in Jewish memory."[317] Jews remember traditionally through myth, not chronologically, per his argument.[318] So, what's the point? The value of historical biographies lies in little more than modern entertainment, often by smearing Jewish historical figures, in sex sells, and in guess work. They represent neither academic scholarship nor the Jewish tradition.

---

[311] Jay Howard Geller, *The Scholems: A Story of the German-Jewish Bourgeoisie from Emancipation to Destruction* (Ithaca, NY: Cornell University Press, 2019), 1.
[312] https://criticaltheoriesofantisemitism.net/jay-geller-profile/. Accessed August 23, 2023.
[313] Geller, *The Scholems*, 6.
[314] Geller, *The Scholems*, 2.
[315] Christopher L. Schilling, "Review of Jay Howard Geller, *The Scholems: A Story of the German-Jewish Bourgeoisie from Emancipation to Destruction*," *Shofar – Interdisciplinary Journal of Jewish Studies* 38.1 (2020): 295–298.
[316] https://criticaltheoriesofantisemitism.net/. Accessed August 23, 2023.
[317] Raphael Patai, "Review of Yosef Hayim Yerushalmi. *Zakhor: Jewish History and Jewish Memory*," *The American Historical Review* 88.5 (1983): 1239; https://doi.org/10.1086/ahr/88.5.1239.
[318] Yosef Hayim Yerushalmi, *Zakhor: Jewish History and Jewish Memory* (Seattle: University of Washington Press, 1982).

Since biographies often do not substantially add to our understanding of history, it does not come as a surprise that adding psychology to the mix creates an even more bizarre picture. Psychohistory is a senseless endeavour, because its theoretical underpinning is psychoanalytic theory, which is, according to the historian David Stannard, "riddled with rippling logical inadequacies."[319] Stannard writes of psychoanalytic theory in *Shrinking History*,

> that any eventuality is covered and can be explained by the presence or absence of the so-called defense mechanisms of reaction-formation, displacement, sublimation, and the like. Although this apparent ability to explain everything has no doubt contributed to the popular appeal of psychoanalysis (as it has with astrology), it flatly disqualifies psychoanalytic theory from any consideration as a theory of scientific or even logically respectable explanation.[320]

Ultimately, "the best modern research now firmly indicates that there are *no* psychological structures established in early childhood that are sufficiently resilient to survive into adulthood without constant environmental support. Moreover, this quality of psychological malleability clearly remains present *after* adulthood is attained."[321] Psychologists might object to this by stating that what has actually happened in one's childhood does not matter, but what the person *thinks* has happened, or has happened beyond one's awareness. Stannard calls this "an approach that not only moves psychoanalytic theory to the realm of the mystical, but that also makes methodologically impossible its transfer to the analysis of historical data."[322] The biologist, science writer, and winner of the 1960 Nobel Prize in Physiology or Medicine, P. B. Medawar, concludes that "psychoanalytic theory is the most stupendous intellectual confidence trick of the twentieth century and a terminal product as well — something akin to a dinosaur or zeppelin in the history of ideas, a vast structure of radically unsound design and with no posterity."[323] But what could possibly be the reason for applying methods that do not even work in their primary function – therapy – to the study of history? In fact, psychohistory is ahistorical according to Stannard:

> Perhaps the single most important achievement of modern historical thinking has been the growing recognition on the part of the historian that life in the past was marked by a fundamental social and cognitive differentness from that prevailing in our own time . . . (concepts of time, space, causation, reality, personhood, sexuality, and the like) . . . It is, therefore, particularly ironical that the fashion of explaining the past by simplistically ap-

---

[319] David Stannard, *Shrinking History: On Freud and the Failure of Psychohistory* (Oxford: Oxford University Press, 1980), 148.
[320] Stannard, *Shrinking History*, 148–149.
[321] Stannard, *Shrinking History*, 149–150; Jerome Kagan et al., *Infancy: Its Place in Human Development* (Cambridge, MA: Harvard University Press, 1978), 113–165.
[322] Stannard, *Shrinking History*, 150.
[323] P. B. Medawar, "Victims of Psychiatry," *The New York Review of Books* 21 (23 January 1975).

plying to it an illogical and ineffective collection of narcissistically contemporary notions should reach such heights just when the best work of an important generation of historians has begun to show how sadly anachronistic any such present-biased explanation system must be.[324]

One way psycho-biographies often work is to "uncover" repressed memory of the person they mentally lay down on their couch. However, there is no such thing as repressed memory. Traumatic events are, as demonstrated by overwhelming scientific evidence, remembered by individuals, no matter whether they suffer from the event or not.[325] On the contrary, we add to our memory rather than repressing it, as the psychologist Elizabeth Loftus has demonstrated with her research into eyewitness memory. Loftus' important work has had an impact on some legal reforms, such as the New Jersey Supreme Court in 2012, which advised judges to instruct juries that eyewitness testimony isn't always reliable.[326] This is important, because "people can be led to remember their past in different ways, and they even can be led to remember entire events that never actually happened to them."[327] In fact, "our memories are constructive. They are reconstructive. Memory works a little bit more like a Wikipedia page: You can go in there and change it, but so can other people."[328] Therapists in particular are to blame here, who often talk their clients into hidden trauma like passive-aggressive hypnotists.

Karen Newirth of the Innocence Project, which helps free people wrongfully convicted of crimes, notes: "Every aspect of what we do to try to prevent eyewitness misidentifications and wrongful convictions can be directly traced to the work that Dr. Loftus has done over the years."[329] And Loftus has come a long way. After she resigned from the American Psychological Association – in part because prominent members of the Association disagreed with her work in 1996 – the association's website came to acknowledge now that most recovered memories are, indeed, not accurate.[330]

---

324 Stannard, *Shrinking History*, 151.
325 Elizabeth Loftus, *The Myth of Repressed Memory: False Memories and Allegations of Sexual Abuse* (New York: St. Martin's Griffin, 1994).
326 https://knowablemagazine.org/article/society/2017/making-case-against-memories-evidence. Accessed August 23, 2023.
327 Elizabeth F. Loftus, and Jacqueline E. Pickell, "The Formation of False Memories," *Psychiatric Annals* 25.12 (1995).
328 https://www.ted.com/talks/elizabeth_loftus_how_reliable_is_your_memory?language=en#t-320055Source:%20https://quotepark.com/quotes/2032612-elizabeth-loftus-memory-works-like-a-wikipedia-page-you-can-go-in/. Accessed August 23, 2023.
329 https://knowablemagazine.org/article/society/2017/making-case-against-memories-evidence. Accessed August 23, 2023.
330 https://www.apa.org/topics/trauma/memories. Accessed August 23, 2023.

In regard to antisemitism, the field of psychohistory has led to the most absurd speculations and scientifically unbacked pseudo-science. R. G. L. Waite saw the Holocaust in his 1971 article, "Adolf Hitler's Guilt Feelings," as a sign of Hitler's projected guilt for having had a Jewish grandfather,[331] which is untrue. The fact is, he was not Jewish. Nor was any bit of his actions a result of his suffering from guilt. Yet this grotesque fantasy (and something that could be misused as an attempt to excuse Nazism) found publication in an academic journal at the time. Walter C. Langer based his study of Hitler on an "anal-erotic hypothesis."[332] Child psychiatrist Robert Coles summarized this absurd study well:

> How did a wretched, deeply troubled, at times pathetic youth—the "neurotic psychopath" of this book—end up Führer of the Third Reich, a man not only possessed of authority and power but believed and heeded by millions? If not Hitler, might it have been someone else? If only Hitler, then surely it was not his "perversion" or his disordered mind (the province of the psychoanalyst) that accounts for his successes . . . The Weimar Republic was full of such people; America has had its share: people who "identify" with various "aggressors"—and, having done so, get nowhere.[333]

Psychohistories, in their attempts to uncover repressed memories from the people they mentally lay down on their couch, do not produce any understanding of antisemites. They are works of fiction. And they can be misused to justify antisemitism because they trivialize human action. The novelist Vladimir Nabokov got it right: "the Freudian faith leads to dangerous ethical consequences, such as when a filthy murderer with the brain of a tapeworm is given a lighter sentence because his mother spanked him too much or too little—it works both ways."[334] The fact that Hitler had not been accepted to art school by a Jewish professor does not explain his antisemitism. Or why did he not also develop hatred towards Scorpios, who treated him badly at some point in his life, or vegetarians (instead of becoming one himself), lefthanders, or any other irrationally fantasised group of evil people? Hitler was affectionate to his dog and liked Wagner operas and flowers from children. Those are facts that can be considered in a biography or a psychological profile about him to paint a full picture of the person. But do they matter when coming to moral or legal judgements of him and his crimes? They do not.

---

331 R. G. L. Waite, "Adolf Hitler's guilt feeling: a problem in history and psychology," *Journal of Interdisciplinary History* 1.2 (1971): 229–249.
332 Walter C. Langer, *The Mind of Adolf Hitler: The Secret Wartime Report* (New York: Basic Books, 1972).
333 Robert Coles, *The Mind's Fate: Ways of Seeing Psychiatry and Psychoanalysis* (Boston: Little, Brown & Co., 1975), 201.
334 Vladimir Nabokov, BBC 2-Interview with Nicholas Garnham, *Strong Opinions*, 99.

Chapter V
Forensic Psychology

The American Psychological Association (APA) defines forensic psychology as "the application of clinical specialties to the legal arena."[335] Therefore, "the practice of forensic psychology, and perhaps the most frequent duty of forensic psychologists," according to the APA, "is the psychological assessment of individuals who are involved, in one way or another, with the legal system."[336] Forensic psychology plays a role in treatment, trial consultations, and research, but most salient here is its assisting law enforcement with criminal profiling and court testimony.

Criminal Profiling

Would psychology help to profile an antisemitic criminal? Despite its popularity in TV shows, movies, true crime podcasts, and the like, compared to untrained individuals, criminal profilers hardly do any better.[337] In one study, they did worse than chemistry majors.[338] The reason why so many still believe there to be any scientific justification for psychological criminal profiling is due mostly the P. T. Barnum Effect[339] – the tendency to see general and vague personality descriptions as believable.[340] What becomes apparent is that their work is more horoscope than science. "Most profilers sprinkle their predictions liberally with assertions that are so nebulous as to be virtually untestable," write Scott O. Lilienfeld et al., "('The killer has unresolved self-esteem problems'), so general that they apply to just about everyone ('The killer has conflicts with his family'), or that rely on base rate information about most crimes ('The killer probably abandoned the body in or near a body of water')."[341] In turn criminal profilers are seen as accurate because many of their

---

335 https://www.apa.org/ed/precollege/psn/2013/09/forensic-psychology. Accessed August 23, 2023.
336 https://www.apa.org/ed/precollege/psn/2013/09/forensic-psychology. Accessed August 23, 2023.
337 R. J. Homant and D. B. Kennedy, "Psychological aspects of crime scene profiling," *Criminal Justice and Behavior* 25 (1998): 319–343.
338 R. N. Kocsis, A. F. Hayes, and H. J. Irwin, "Investigative experience and accuracy in psychological profiling of a violent crime," *Journal of Interpersonal Violence* 17 (2002): 811–823.
339 P. E. Meehl, "Wanted: A good cookbook," *American Psychologist* 11 (1956): 263–272.
340 Malcolm Gladwell, "Dangerous minds: Criminal profiling made easy," *The New Yorker* (12 November 2007) 36–45.
341 Scott O. Lilienfeld, Steven Jay Lynn, John Ruscio, and Barry L. Beyerstein, *50 Great Myths of Popular Psychology: Shattering Widespread Misconceptions about Human Behavior* (Malden, MA: Wiley-Blackwell, 2009), 216.

predictions are hard to disprove or bound to be right.[342] Brent Snook et al. conclude in their research that criminal profiling should not be used as it lacks scientific support, while people have been misled into believing that it works "despite no sound theoretical grounding and no strong empirical support," and that

> Potentially responsible for this illusory belief is the information that people acquire about CP [criminal profiling], which is heavily influenced by anecdotes, repetition of the message that profiling works, the expert profiler label, and a disproportionate emphasis on correct predictions.[343] [brackets added]

David V. Canter et al. point to outdated concepts of little usefulness in criminal profiling, such as "the binary notion of offenders belonging to organised or disorganised trait sub-types, and that such traits can be predictive of offence mechanisms."[344] And David Wilson, professor of criminology at Birmingham City University, argues with two of his colleagues from its psychology department that until criminal profiling "is more formally verified, the evidential usefulness of profiles should be treated cautiously, or even entirely excluded from consideration in court."[345] Thus, as important as it is to predict antisemitic criminals' behavior, psychology does little or nothing to assist with this.

Court Testimony

Psychologists also help in courtroom settings to mitigate sentencing or to force people into psychiatric treatment, as such people could commit a crime in the future based on their mental illness. But according to the rule of law – which Western countries rightly pride themselves with upholding – one must be punished for what he or she has done, not what they might do at some future point in life. The incorporation of psychology into the determination of the sentences therefore undermines the rule of law. The fact that this is happening on the basis of a

---

342 L. J. Alison, M. D. Smith, O. Eastman, and L. Rainbow, "Toulmin's philosophy of argument and its relevance to offender profiling," *Psychology, Crime, and Law* 9 (2003): 173–183.
343 Brent Snook, R. M. Cullen, C. Bennell, P. J. Taylor, and P. Gendreau, "The Criminal Profiling Illusion: What's Behind the Smoke and Mirrors?" *Criminal Justice and Behavior* 35.10 (2008): 1257–1276. https://doi.org/10.1177/0093854808321528.
344 David V. Canter, L. J. Alison, E. Alison, N. and Wentink, "The organized/disorganized typology of serial murder: Myth or model?" *Psychology, Public Policy, and Law* 10 (2004): 293–320.
345 Craig Jackson, David Wilson, and Baljit Kaur Rana, "The usefulness of criminal profiling," *Criminal Justice Matters* 84.1 (2011): 7; doi: 10.1080/09627251.2011.576014; see also D. Wilson, C. A. Jackson, and B. Rana, "Against the medical- psychological tradition of understanding serial killing by studying the killers: The case of BTK," *Amicus Journal* 22 (2010): 8–16.

science that is at the least deeply flawed, or outright pseudo-science,[346] is even the more tragic. "An expert in a court room setting is supposed to be competent to present an opinion with reasonable certainty. But a mental health expert who expresses a confident opinion about the probable future behavior of a single individual (for example, to engage in violent acts) is by definition incompetent," writes the mathematical psychologist Robyn M. Dawes,

> because the research has demonstrated that neither a mental health expert nor anyone else can make such a prediction with accuracy sufficient to warrant much confidence. (Professionals often state that their professional role "requires" them to make such judgments, however much they personally appreciate the uncertainty involved. No, they are not required—they volunteer.)[347]

Of course, nor are they required to determine if a convicted criminal is "irredeemable" and thus eligible for execution, one may add. Fortunately, at least Israel's regional psychiatrists (who are responsible for civil commitment decisions in their districts) "have become more lenient and do not issue commitment orders for patients whose actions may have warranted involuntary hospitalization in the past," observes Deputy Director of the Lev Hasharon Mental Health Center, Yuval Melamed.[348]

The argument against this would be that psychologists are not undermining the rule of law but are part of the process as licenced experts. But the fact that psychologists are "no better as psychotherapists than are others of comparable intelligence who are minimally trained" and "do not have any special abilities in diagnosing mental distress and predicting human behavior, or in evaluating what causes particular people to behave and feel as they do," as Dawes has explained,[349] raises questions regarding the legal justification of licencing "psychologists." If psychology is

---

[346] See, for instance, Tomasz Witkowski and Maciej Zatonski, *Psychology Gone Wrong: The Dark Sides of Science and Therapy* (Boca Raton, FL: Brown Walker Press, 2015); Tomasz Witkowski, *Psychology Led Astray: Cargo Cult in Science and Therapy*, (Boca Raton, FL: Brown Walker Press, 2016); Tomasz Witkowski, *Shaping Psychology: Perspectives on Legacy, Controversy and the Future of the Field* (New York: Palgrave Macmillan, 2020); Jeffrey Moussaieff Masson, *Against Therapy: Emotional Tyranny and the Myth of Psychological Healing* (New York: Athenaeum, 1988); Theodore Dalrymple, *Admirable Evasions: How Psychology Undermines Morality* (New York: Encounter Books, 2015); on the pseudo-scientific nature of Freud's work, see, for instance, Karl Popper, *The Logic of Scientific Discovery* (London: Routledge, 1959); Frederick Crews, *Freud: The Making of an Illusion* (New York: Metropolitan Books, 2017).
[347] Theodore Dalrymple, *Admirable Evasions: How Psychology Undermines Morality* (New York: Encounter Books, 2015), viii.
[348] Yuval Melamed, "Mentally Ill Persons Who Commit Crimes: Punishment or Treatment?" *Journal of the American Academy of Psychiatry and the Law* 38.1 (2010): 100–103.
[349] Dawes, *House of Cards*, 13.

not more effective in its treatments than are those administered by non-trained people, licencing it would be a restraint of trade. The reason for licencing it is that patients need protection. This certainly applies to situations in which psychologists have institutional power (prisons, nursing homes, the military, etc.), and in which the state has the right – and the obligation – to make sure those in power are qualified in terms of educational background and professional conduct. But apparently the psychological background can't guarantee this, which is why the state must consider better ways to limit the abuse of power by caretakers. Outside of these institutional settings, the question of a legal justification of licencing treatment by intellectually competent people is even less clear. After all, we do not license (i.e. regulate) advice-giving in free societies, as can be seen with the emergence of the most outrageous self-help and diet books on the market. This leaves one with a justification: licencing psychologists helps clients to evaluate services available on the market. But, of course, this would be a weak argument, as people who are legally competent enough to choose psychological services should not require assistance to choose between equally effective services. And the problem with this argument is, according to Dawes,

> that the education and training psychologists receive is not necessarily training in valid techniques or theories, but far too often is training in the opinion of someone with high status, opinion that may or may not have any scientific basis. This person in turn achieved status by being trained in the opinion of a previous high-status person. The student goes on to achieve high status as the result of the training and may later train someone else in the same opinion (usually slightly modified), and so on and so on. With a little bit of luck, or with planning on the part of the more responsible training programs, there is some scientific foundation somewhere in this self-perpetuating process. Otherwise, there is none.[350]

Dawes concludes that "licensing, which leads to the pretense of scientifically based knowledge where none exists, does not assure quality"[351] and refers to the acclaimed psychologist Lee Sechrest, who points out that a license implies expertise in whatever the licensed person has been trained to do within the domain of psychology:

> Court testimony is an example of what has happened. We [psychologists] drifted into it as a field. It started with psychologists talking about matters where they did have some expertise: measurement of intellectual functioning, descriptions of cognitive and behavioral impairment, and so on. Now psychologists can be "expert" on anything that can be defined as "psychology." That doesn't follow. Just because there are all sorts of things that are part psychological in nature — they involve behavior, beliefs, attitudes and so on — doesn't mean

---

350 Dawes, *House of Cards*, 139–140.
351 Dawes, *House of Cards*, 142.

that we can claim to be experts in an area that involves these things without having to generate a scientific data base.[352] [brackets added]

When legislators came up with licensures for psychology, they certainly had in mind that psychology was a science, whose practice should be licensed, like the practise of engineering or medicine. And that it would require practitioners to be disciplined by science. The result, however, is a licence to present science and themselves as experts of it, and that even in legal settings.

Psychologists are often impactful (in the legal process), because ultimately they agree with the rest of us on what is normal and what sticks out as "sick." Indeed, what a "sick man" the Halimi killer must be to be an antisemite and to commit such a horrific crime. But such a common view of crime and personal character gets presented by psychologists as scientific discovery, about which they in their professional opinions refer to each other as authority figures. And by doing so, common perspective becomes the evasion of individual responsibility. One does not need a psychiatric evaluation to see that it is not normal human behaviour to enter the apartment of a stranger at night, torture her, and throw the victim out of her window. To understand the "sickness" of the act does not make one an authority over the law. Or at least it should not.

Psychological assessments take away the tragedy (and the glory) of being human, which means constantly having to decide what is right and what is wrong, and being responsible for these very decisions. But the notion of people committing crimes because they are unhealthy has entered more and more into the law of many Western countries, not just France. The question is now less about whether people do wrong knowingly or not, but whether they are healthy or not. Psychology, therefore, does not help in the sentencing of antisemitic criminals. On the contrary, it often leads to horrific injustice while undermining the rule of law, as the Halimi murder has demonstrated so shockingly.

Tolstoy put it best in *The Devil* when his protagonist Yevgeny Irtenev murdered an old affair, is put to trial, and the jury decides it was a case of temporary insanity (after waiting for the trial, he only receives church penance of a month): "And indeed, if Yevgeny Irtenev was mentally deranged when he committed this crime, then everyone is similarly insane. The most mentally deranged people are certainly those who see in others indications of insanity they do not notice in

---

352 S. C. Hayes, "An Interview with Lee Sechrest: The Courage to Say 'We Do Not Know How,'" *APS Observer* 2.4 (1989): 9.

themselves."³⁵³ Deciding "not to judge the mad" in the case of the Halimi killer, because he was undergoing a "psychotic episode" due to cannabis consumption, is insanity, deranged, and unjust. Not he, but rather those psychological experts and judges are in need of treatment, as they have exchanged responsibility and morality for mental health.

In principle, the insanity defence was reasonable when it became part of legal rulings. The *McNaghten's Case* of 1843 established the customary test of insanity in Anglo-American criminal proceedings by finding people who understand common conceptions of reality (especially what society understands as right and wrong) as responsible for their actions.³⁵⁴ Therefore this landmark ruling found the mentally incompetent not to be guilty of a crime by reason of insanity. In their Enlightenment argumentation, the judges found that

> to establish a defence on the ground of insanity, it must be clearly proved that, at the time of the committing of the act, the party accused as labouring under such a defect of reason, from disease of the mind, as not to know the nature and quality of the act he was doing; or, if he did know it, that he did not know he was doing what was wrong.³⁵⁵

This right-or-wrong test was later supplemented in the United States by the "irresistible impulse" test, designed to ensure that people could not be ruled guilty of a crime by reasons of "irresistible impulse." But is it as simple as this: anyone as crazy enough to fall for antisemitism must be crazy? And are we able to distinguish between resistible impulses and irresistible ones? Since the distinction is impossible, judges and juries turn to the psychological and psychiatric authorities. They, in turn, may disagree on specific matters (depending often on who writes the check).³⁵⁶ Identifying and managing potential bias in forensic evaluations is a known problem.³⁵⁷ And evaluations usually confirm the psychologist's subjective preferences and loyalties to a particular theory, regardless of number

---

353 Leo Tolstoy, *The Devil and other Short Stories* (trans. Louise and Aylmer Maude; Oxford: Oxford University Press, 2012). The quote stems from Tolstoy's alternative conclusion to *The Devil*.
354 https://www.britannica.com/topic/MNaghtens-Case. Accessed August 23, 2023.
355 https://www.britannica.com/topic/MNaghtens-Case. Accessed August 23, 2023.
356 Dawes, *House of Cards*, 230.
357 R. Borum, R. Otto, and S. Golding, "Improving clinical judgment and decision making in forensic evaluation," *The Journal of Psychiatry & Law* 21 (1993): 35–76; D. Faust, *Coping with psychiatric and psychological testimony* (6th ed.; New York: Oxford University Press, 2012); P. Croskerry, "Achieving Quality in Clinical Decision Making: Cognitive Strategies and Detection of Bias," *Academic Emergency Medicine Journal* 9 (2012): 1184–1204; N. Z. Hilton, G. T. Harris, and M. E. Rice, "Sixty-six years of research on the clinical versus actuarial prediction of violence," *The Counseling Psychologist* 34 (2006): 400–409.

of years of experience.[358] This is commonly referred to as the "allegiance bias" or "allegiance effect." This effect not only manifest itself in research results but also in the courtroom. As a solution, psychologists have promoted awareness of the problem. Yet studies indicate that being aware of the bias has little to no corrective effect.[359] At a loss for options, psychologists now call for "awareness and commitment."[360]

As Dawes states, "there is no knowledge in psychiatry or psychology that would allow anyone to determine whether impulses are 'irresistible'—no theory, no valid assessment technique, no evidence of special intuitive discrimination powers of 'trained clinicians,' nothing."[361] Even a former president of the American Psychiatric Association, and professor of law and psychiatry, found that "his colleagues who confidently make this distinction in court are best regarded as "'a bunch of clowns.'"[362]

And the whole matter increasingly becomes a "clown show" as more and more people in society see themselves not as having experienced terrible hardships in life but as having suffered from mental illnesses and having become victims of those. Those claims are important, because definitions of legal insanity develop to reflect changes in medical understandings and societal attitudes in regard to mental health.[363] Legal scholars Lisa Claydon and Paul Catley argue in *Law and Mind: A Survey of Law and the Cognitive Sciences* that "from the beginning the insanity defence was politically charged,"[364] while law professor Christopher Slobogin writes: "The insanity defense is perhaps the most widely discussed

---

[358] W. M. Grove, D. H. Zald, B. S. Lebow, B. E. Snitz, and C. Nelson, "Clinical vs. mechanical prediction: A meta-analysis," *Psychological Assessment* 12 (2000): 19–30; I. E. Sladeczek, F. Dumont, C. A. Martel, and A. Karagiannakis, "Making sense of client data: Clinical experience and confirmation revisited," *American Journal of Psychotherapy* 60 (2006): 375–391.

[359] R. P. Larrick, "Debiasing," in D. J. Koehler and N. Harvey (eds.), *Blackwell Handbook of Judgment and Decision Making* (Malden, MA: Blackwell, 2004), 316–337; R. S. Nickerson, *Cognition and chance: The psychology of probabilistic reasoning* (Mahwah, NJ: Lawrence Erlbaum Associates, 2004).

[360] https://www.apadivisions.org/division-41/publications/newsletters/news/2014/10/expert-opinion. Accessed August 23, 2023.

[361] Dawes, *House of Cards*, 230.

[362] Dawes, *House of Cards*, 230.

[363] L. Claydon and P. Catley, "Thoughts on the Insanity Defence," in B. Brożek, J. Hage, and N. Vincent (eds.), *Law and Mind: A Survey of Law and the Cognitive Sciences* (Cambridge: Cambridge University Press, 2021), 342–350; R. D. Mackay, *Mental Condition Defences in the Criminal Law* (Oxford: Clarendon, 1995); S. Moratti and D. Patterson, eds., *Legal Insanity and the Brain: Science, Law and European Courts* (Oxford: Hart, 2016); M. D. White, ed., *The Insanity Defense: Multidisciplinary Views on Its History, Trends and Controversies* (Santa Barbara: Praeger, 2017).

[364] Claydon and Catley, "Thoughts on the Insanity Defence," 342.

doctrine in criminal law."[365] Major debates surround the question of how reliable information gathered retrospectively, after a crime has taken place, can be. After all, a defendant could be in a different mental condition during the examination than at the time of the act. Another concern is the fact that a defendant may fake insanity. And with the insanity defence being at least a possibility, people might be incentivised to commit crimes inasmuch as they feel they could get away with it.

Hence, critical opposition to forensic psychiatric testimony in the courtroom is nothing new. Harvard law professor Alan A. Stone voiced his opposition at the Thirteenth Annual Meeting of the American Academy of Psychiatry and the Law in 1982:

> I am not a forensic psychiatrist. What has kept me out of the courtroom is my concern about the ethical boundaries of forensic psychiatry. Let me state what I think the ethical boundary problems are. First, there is the basic boundary question. Does psychiatry have anything true to say that the courts should listen to? Second, there is the risk that one will go too far and twist the rules of justice and fairness to help the patient. Third, there is the opposite risk that one will deceive the patient in order to serve justice and fairness. Fourth, there is the danger that one will prostitute the profession, as one is alternately seduced by the power of the adversarial system and assaulted by it. Finally, as one struggles with these four issues – Does one have something true to say? Is one twisting justice? Is one deceiving the patient? Is one prostituting the profession? – there is the additional problem: forensic psychiatrists are without any clear guidelines as to what is proper and ethical, at least as far as I can see.[366]

Psychologists mostly disturb the legal process. As discussed, false memories can be implanted in anyone. Hence the psychologist Paul Moloney argues that "this phenomenon, controversially, may have led to miscarriages of justice, when vague or distant (and unsubstantiated) childhood recollections disclosed by adult patients in the consulting room have been transmuted into supposedly unquestionable legal evidence."[367] On the other hand, psychologists such as Elizabeth Loftus are much needed in the legal process to correct this error and to remind that most recovered memories are not accurate.

---

365 Christopher Slobogin, "Introduction to this Special Issue: The Characteristics of Insanity and the Insanity Evaluation Process," *Behavioral Sciences and the Law* 36.3 (2018): 271–275. doi: https://doi.org/10.1002/bsl.2342.
366 Quoted in Gerben Meynen, "The Insanity Defense," in B. Brożek, J. Hage, and N. Vincent (eds.), *Law and Mind: A Survey of Law and the Cognitive Sciences* (Cambridge: Cambridge University Press, 2021), 331–332.
367 Moloney, *The Therapy Industry*, 57.

But are there any examples of good legal practise? Is there a light at the end of the lunatic asylum corridor, so to speak?[368] Two examples from two different countries and times come to mind here. On March 20, 1995, the Japanese doomsday cult *Aum Shinrikyo* (now called *Aleph*) carried out its sarin attack on the Tokyo subway. Two months prior to the terrorist attack, the cult published an extremely antisemitic tract called "Manual of Fear: The Jewish Ambition – Total World Conquest." In the tract, *Aum* claimed that the Jews had taken advantage of Japan's devastation after World War II as a step in their conspiracy to achieve total world domination. Prior to the attack, the cult had also published an enemy list, including Japanese people, whom they labelled the "Jewish Japanese."[369] While Article 39 of Japan's Criminal Law recognizes that "an incompetent person shall not be punished; a person with diminished competence shall be given a mitigation of punishment," in practise this is only rarely applied. Consequently, the terrorist cult leader was not successful in his insanity defence when he had to stand trial. He was found guilty and sentenced to death. Yet, the decision to find him guilty did not come as a surprise given Japan's system of prosecution, with its suspiciously high conviction rates. While critics argue that some of the Imperial-era practices still prevail in the Japanese criminal justice system, it also seems questionable to offer Japan as a role model to the West in this regard.

Another more famous example is the Eichmann trial in Jerusalem. During the trial, prosecutor Gideon Hausner called on Gustave Gilbert to take the witness stand as a psychological authority. Gilbert, Professor and Chair of the Psychology Department of Long Island University ("perhaps, the most qualified expert in the world")[370] had been prison psychologist at the Nuremberg Trials of the Major War Criminals in 1946. Hausner wanted Gilbert to report on his conversations in Nuremberg, as well as to provide the court with his assessment of the psychological tests administered to Eichmann by Shlomo Kulcsar (a psychiatrist and Head of the Psychiatric Department at Tel Hashomer Hospital) and evaluated by his wife Shoshanna (the chief clinical psychologist in the Psychiatric Department at the same hospital), and to settle the question of whether Eichmann had been capable of committing the crimes for which he was put to trial. Moshe Landau, the Presiding Judge, however, refused to admit the statement on the ground that the trial "was to deal not with Eichmann's capacity to commit crimes, but with the ques-

---

368 A brilliant phrase I took from one of the anonymous reviewers of this book.
369 Christopher L. Schilling, "Buddhist Anti-Semitism," *Jewish Political Studies Review* 31.3–4 (22 February 2021).
370 Quoted in José Brunner, "Eichmann's Mind: Psychological, Philosophical, and Legal Perspectives," *Tel Aviv University Law School Faculty Papers* 61 (2008): 23.

tion of whether Eichmann actually had committed the acts attributed to him,"[371] writes José Brunner in his examination of the court proceedings. And "Since psychological expertise could not contribute to the clarification of the latter issue, such expert testimony could not be permitted."[372] Though Gilbert eventually testified, he did not as a psychological authority.[373] Judge Landau was wise in his restrictive approach, and avoided controversy. It should have become an example.

As "whimsical"[374] and "dubious"[375] as some of the Kulcsar's tests conducted on Eichmann were, they are certainly a captivating tale of the quest to understand human behavior in its most horrific form. Despite all flaws, what is admittedly honourable about psychology is its intense interest in humans with everything that comes with that. And it can be helpful when psychology reminds one of the human nature behind legal processes and judge's decision-making processes. There has been quite promising research by a group of Israeli researchers on the correlation between when judges had eaten and their tendencies in decision-making, for instance.[376] When judging and punishing (antisemitic) crimes, trivial parts of human nature such as hunger must be considered, and psychology with its interest in human behavior reminds us of this. If psychology seeks to retain any kind of justifiable place within the law, then it should be here, where it can point to biases in human decision making. Otherwise, what psychology does in courtrooms is to find excuses on the grounds of false "scientific" findings, which do not help to prevent the problem but rather may help the guilty evade responsibility.

The history of criminology and court practice is full of methods which were once considered valid and reliable but either had to be abandoned or came seriously into question – be it phrenology or graphology in the past, or Field Sobriety Tests and certain applications of canines detection of potential suspects in the present.[377] Every scientist or forensic expert must always be ready to question the accuracy of the tools she uses, just as any craftsman needs to keep his tools in good condition. Lacking evidence that they can offer any insight, psychologists

---

371 Brunner, "Eichmann's Mind," 23.
372 *The Trial of Adolf Eichmann: Record of Proceedings in the District Court of Jerusalem* (Jerusalem: Trust for the Publication of the Proceedings of the Eichmann Trial, 1992–1993), 1009–1010.
373 Brunner, "Eichmann's Mind," 23.
374 Brunner, "Eichmann's Mind," 27.
375 Brunner, "Eichmann's Mind," 27.
376 Shai Danziger, Jonathan Levav, and Liora Avnaim-Pesso, "Extraneous Factors in Judicial Decisions," *Proceedings of the National Academy of Sciences of the United States of America* 108.17 (2011): 6889–6892; see http://www.pnas.org/content/108/17/6889.full.pdf+html. Accessed August 23, 2023.
377 I'm thankful to one of the anonymous reviewers for pointing me to this.

should be thrown out of court rooms, and new legal tests of responsibility that do not include pseudo-scientific findings should be developed.

Ultimately the question is: do we view humans as biochemical machines that have to be psychologically regulated and pharmaceutically adjusted, or as beings that to some extent exercise free will and are responsible for their actions? But this is, of course, a false choice, because one cannot fundamentally change the human mind and heart via psychological interventions or pharmaceuticals. The human mind is nothing like this. We either follow the myth and live in the dangerous delusion that we can do so, or we face the reality of human responsibility.

Chapter VI
Psychology and Policymaking

Pennsylvania Supreme Court Judge David Wecht stated after the shooting in Pittsburgh's Tree of Life Synagogue:

> For a time after the Holocaust, the sheer horror and magnitude of the slaughter tended to tamp down the most vocal anti-Semites. But something's changed both on the right and the left. People are increasingly willing to voice anti-Semitic sentiments. And when people, particularly leaders, don't publicly oppose anti-Jewish speech, hatred against Jews festers and grows. And that's why I think this is a critical time in America.[378]

Judge Wecht is right about this. But it is also a critical moment as people, and particularly leaders, are increasingly misunderstanding antisemitism by relying on pseudo-science. Not speaking up against it is one thing. It is another thing entirely to look to the most absurd places – from the birth canal and bad parenting to a victim's behaviour – in search of any kind of excuse or explanation. And it is not only in America that this is happening.

Psychologists are academics and mostly speak with extreme confidence about their ideas and methods; they give public lectures, write books and articles, and ultimately become authority figures in society. Consequently, the belief that psychology offers a tool to understand antisemitism has become a part of policymaking, too. In May 2023, the White House issued the "U.S. National Strategy to Counter Antisemitism" and wrote under "Executive Branch Actions": "The National Science Foundation (NSF) will reach out to the scientific research community ... NSF will encourage diverse research on hate through developmental, cognitive, social psychological, and sociological approaches."[379] In 2006, Avner Falk wrote for the Jerusalem Center for Public Affairs, an Israeli think tank, that "although, like social-science and human-science theories in general, psychoanalytic theories cannot be tested with the same rigor as natural-science theories, they can help illuminate such crucial human issues as war and peace, politics, racism, anti-Semitism, and genocide."[380] Unfortunately, there is little evidence for this having been the case, at the time of his article's writing or since.

---

[378] Joel Cohen, "Pennsylvania Judge David N. Wecht talks about anti-Semitism," *Pittsburgh Jewish Chronicle* (12 April 2019).
[379] https://www.whitehouse.gov/wp-content/uploads/2023/05/U.S.-National-Strategy-to-Counter-Antisemitism.pdf. Accessed August 23, 2023.
[380] Avner Falk, "Collective Psychological Processes in Anti-Semitism," *Jewish Political Studies Review* 18.1–2 (2006).

And psychology's tendency to think, rather eccentrically, outside the box can mislead scholars and policymakers into unhelpful mix-ups. Singapore is a country that does surprisingly well in many regards, one being its relatively low level of antisemitism. The Anti-Defamation League marked its level of antisemitism at 16 percent in their 2014 survey,[381] in comparison to China (20 percent),[382] Japan (23 percent),[383] and South Korea (53 percent).[384] This is quite a remarkable fact, given that those countries are of the same larger regions yet do not have any significant Muslim population, like Singapore does.[385] A reason for this success seem to be policy decisions, such as the implementation of Singapore's Maintenance of Religious Harmony Act, with its radical stance on the punishment of religious offenses.[386] Luca Farrow is a British lawyer and a thoughtful research analyst at a Singapore government think-tank and research institute which is part of the country's prestigious Nanyang Technological University. But when he incorporates psychology into his policy analysis, he greatly misunderstands antisemitism and Islamophobia to be "fundamentally similar" and tries to counter both by focusing on prejudice and in-group/out-group dynamics,[387] a policy recommendation that would certainly not help Singapore to improve further.

---

[381] https://global100.adl.org/country/singapore/2014. Accessed August 23, 2023.

[382] https://global100.adl.org/country/china/2014. Accessed August 23, 2023.

[383] https://global100.adl.org/country/japan/2014. Accessed August 23, 2023.

[384] https://global100.adl.org/country/south-korea/2014; Accessed August 23, 2023. See also Christopher L. Schilling, "Jewish Seoul: An Analysis of Philo- and Antisemitism in South Korea," *Modern Judaism – A Journal of Jewish Ideas and Experience* 38.2 (2018): 183–197, https://doi.org/10.1093/mj/kjy002.

[385] The ADL leadership has certainly become a "lightning rod for vicious criticism from both the left and the right" in recent years, and often for good reason. But one should differentiate here between the poor quality of certain leadership decisions in terms of public advocacy, and ADL's interesting polling work, which despite its flaws points to something interesting. See: https://www.haaretz.com/opinion/2018-05-03/ty-article-opinion/.premium/from-left-and-right-why-is-a-league-of-haters-descending-on-the-adl/0000017f-f8ec-ddde-abff-fced79930000. Accessed September 10, 2023.

[386] The legal scholar and sociologist George Baylon Radics is a fantastic source for understanding the tension between freedom of speech and laws restricting the defamation of religion in Singapore. See George Baylon Radics and Vineeta Sinha, "Regulation of Religion and Granting of Public Holidays: The Case of Tai Pucam in Singapore," *Asian Journal of Social Science* 46.4–5 (2018); George Baylon Radics and Poon Yee Suan, "Amos Yee, Free Speech, and Maintaining Religious Harmony in Singapore," *University of Pennsylvania Asian Law Review* 12.2 (2016).

[387] https://www.rsis.edu.sg/rsis-publication/rsis/islamophobia-and-antisemitism-in-sg-narratives-of-grievance/; Accessed August 23, 2023. The Website states: "Luca Farrow is a Research Analyst with the Studies in Inter-Religious Relations in Plural Societies (SRP) Programme, S. Rajaratnam School of International Studies (RSIS), Nanyang Technological University, Singapore" *and* "RSIS Commentary is a platform to provide timely and, where appropriate, policy-relevant commen-

An unhelpful mix up of categories and topics while using psychology as a policy recommendation against antisemitism can be found on the other side of the world, too. This is especially so in Germany these days. In 2021, under the headline "Psychologists must have more impact on German society," the APA called for psychologists to "use their expertise to recommend actions to political decision makers."[388] Samuel Salzborn has been affiliated with the Center for Research on Antisemitism (ZfA) at TU Berlin as well as other German universities that have not faced such a high level of controversy and justified criticism, unlike the ZfA.[389] He is a strong advocate for assessing antisemitism through the lens of psy-

---

tary and analysis of topical and contemporary issues. The authors' [Luca Farrow] views are their own and do not represent the official position of the S. Rajaratnam School of International Studies (RSIS), NTU."

[388] www.apa.org/international/global-insights/psychologists-german-society. Accessed August 23, 2023.

[389] For equating Islamophobia with antisemitism, see: https://www.wsj.com/articles/SB122869182286886467; Its current director, Stefanie Schüler-Springorum, spoke in this regard about "controversy" herself. See: https://www.deutschlandfunkkultur.de/mitten-in-der-kontroverse-100.html (Access date: October 24, 2023). For downplaying antisemitism, see: https://www.welt.de/politik/deutschland/plus212227173/Wolfgang-Benz-Und-ploetzlich-soll-Du-Jude-nicht-mehr-antisemitisch-sein.html (Access date October 21, 2023); For "equating Islamophobia with anti-Semitism while ignoring Iran's genocidal threats toward Israel and trivializing the Holocaust", see: https://www.jpost.com/iranian-threat/news/german-center-ignores-iranian-threat (Access date October 21, 2023); For being reluctant to address Islamic or Islamist antisemitism and to argue that doing so is either unjustified or counterproductive. See: Jeffrey Herf. Review of *Nazis und der Nahe Osten: Wie der Islamische Antisemitismus Entstand*, by Matthias Küntzel. *Antisemitism Studies* 5, no. 1 (2021): 218–229. By its students see: https://www.juedische-allgemeine.de/kultur/studierende-kritisieren-zentrum-fuer-antisemitismusforschung/ (Access date October 20, 2023); For failing to address radical left-wing, communist and Islamic Jew-hatred, See: https://www.jpost.com/diaspora/antisemitism/us-expert-berlin-antisemitism-center-ignores-israel-related-antisemitism-623073 (Access date October 20, 2023). Critique of the Center by the *Jerusalem Post* and *Haaretz* were called by it "tirades of hatred" (*Hasstiraden*) and motivated by money. See: https://www.tu-berlin.de/fileadmin/i65/Newsletter/news-09-01.pdf. (Access date October 20, 2023); The American Jewish Committee accused the Center of a "trivialization of antisemitism", see: https://www.welt.de/kultur/article137319779/Deutsche-Forscher-schaffen-Antisemitismus-ab.html (Access date October 20, 2023); Regarding its research project on "Jewish Pimps", see footnotes chapter 1; The Center has also published a chapter by Meron Medzini (see footnotes chapter 1). See: https://www.static.tu.berlin/fileadmin/www/10002032/Jahrbuecher/Jahrbuch_2021.pdf (Access date October 20, 2023); For a critique on its involvement and marketing of the Jerusalem Declaration on Antisemitism, see: Steinberg, Gerald M.. "The Central Political Role of German Left Actors in the Campaign to Replace the IHRA Working Definition of Antisemitism", *Journal of Contemporary Antisemitism* 5, no. 2 (2022): 67–82; For not seeing antisemitism studies as integral part of Jewish studies, see: Gideon Botsch and Christoph Kopke. "'Im Grunde genommen sollten wir schweigen...': Jüdische Studien ohne Antisemitismus - Antisemitismusforschung ohne Juden?", in: "*...und handle mit*

chology,[390] and he eventually became the official "Contact Person for Antisemitism"[391] of Berlin in 2020.

The questionable "Antisemitism Commissioner" for the southern-German state of Baden-Württemberg, Michael Blume, evidences the same kinds of leanings when it comes to psychology.[392] The Simon Wiesenthal Center has on the basis of his social media activity put him on their "Global Anti-Semitism 2021 Top Ten List" in place 7 (behind Hamas in place 2 and Iran in place 1).[393] In 2022, Blume, himself of a non-Jewish background, also spoke in an article of some Jews having a "massive problem with non-Jews,"[394] and in an interview with a German radio station he spoke of his critics as "hateful" and identified among them "right-wing extremist" members of Jewish communities in Germany [*rechtsextrem*, a German term commonly used for neo-Nazis].[395] Tellingly, the Israeli-German Professor Emeritus of modern history, Michael Wolffsohn, understands him not to be an antisemite, but concludes: "Blume is a ‹useful idiot› of the antisemites."[396] Yet in October 2022, a court in Hamburg exonerated a journalist for calling the commissioner himself an "antisemite" given the "sufficient facts" pointing to it.[397]

Vernunft- *Beiträge zur europäisch-jüdischen Beziehungsgeschichte,* Festschrift zum 20 jährigen Bestehen des Moses Mendelssohn Zentrums, Hildesheim/Zürich/New York 2012, pp. 303–320; The Center seems to welcome psychological research on antisemitism beyond Salzborn's work. See: https://www.tu.berlin/asf/ueber-uns/team/fellows/prof-dr-ilka-quindeau (Access date October 21, 2023).
390 Samuel Salzborn, "Zur Politischen Psychologie des Antisemitismus," *Journal für Psychologie* 18.1 (2010): 1.
391 *Ansprechpartner des Landes Berlin zu Antisemitismus.*
392 Blume has been appointed after consultations with Jewish community representatives in his state. It must be noted, though, that one could argue that the majority of Jews in Germany are not currently (active) members of these communities (fortunately there is no official data on where or what Jews do in Germany anymore), and that the German state funds its religious institutions, including the Jewish ones, which it consults on the matter.
393 https://www.wiesenthal.com/assets/pdf/global_anti-semitism_2021_top_ten.pdf. Accessed August 23, 2023.
394 https://scilogs.spektrum.de/natur-des-glaubens/verschwoerungsfragen-46-ueber-impfungen-und-erwaehlung-im-judentum/. Accessed August 23, 2023.
395 https://www.deutschlandfunk.de/pandemischer-antisemitismus-was-antisemitismusbeauftrage-dagegen-tun-dlf-51e99ecc-100.html. Accessed August 23, 2023.
396 "Blume ist ein ‹nützlicher Idiot› der Antisemiten." see: https://www.nzz.ch/international/kann-ein-antisemitismusbeauftragter-ein-antisemit-sein-ld.1662424. Accessed August 23, 2023.
397 https://www.welt.de/politik/deutschland/plus241813857/Michael-Blume-Antisemitismus-Beauftragter-darf-antisemitisch-genannt-werden.html; Accessed August 23, 2023. I am not aware of Blume's response to this judgement.

Blume, a political scientist with a degree in religious studies, claimed in interviews that we can understand antisemitism only once we deal with the psychological mechanism behind it.[398] This position is either a foolish denial of reality or a strangely aggressive naïveté. Antisemitism is exactly what psychology *cannot* explain.

In my impression of their policymaking, Blume's and Salzborn's work has done little to fight antisemitism in Germany so far.[399] Apart from recommending the renaming of streets in Berlin, Salzborn apparently saw his role as a call to defend the Covid-19 policy of the German government against opposition, which he saw as a "classic mass psychological group phenomenon."[400] Yet, as right or as wrong as certain German Covid-19 policies may have been, the two topics simply do not belong together. And people are either right about their protests or they are wrong, but certainly they are not blindly following some mass phenomenon that frees them of any personal agency. His confused and dangerous mix-up of topics could even have prompted antisemitism, as he may have been misunderstood by some to be advocating the odd idea that certain Covid-19 restrictions were necessary to protect Jews, and thus turning pandemic frustrations in Germany into antisemitic sentiment. A picture of him from a newspaper interview in front of the New Synagogue in Berlin speaking out against protestors of the Covid-19 policies did certainly not help.[401]

Nor did Blume's mixed-up of antisemitism with climate change. In an official report on how to fight antisemitism, he wrote:

> If we want to credibly fight antisemitism globally and stand up for democracy and the rule of law, then this must also mean greater efforts for the transition to renewable energies and decarbonization. The burning of fossil raw materials not only poisons the environment and climate, but also deforms societies, states and religious teachings into authoritarianism. At the same time, there is already a risk of new dependencies expanding, for example in the

---

398 See, for instance, https://www.domradio.de/artikel/eine-umgedrehte-religion-religionswissenschaftler-blume-analysiert-verschwoerungsmythen; Accessed August 23, 2023. https://www.konradsblatt.de/aktuell-2/detail/nachricht-seite/id/150049-antisemitismus-ist-ein-krisensymptom/?default=true; Accessed August 23, 2023. https://www.evangelische-aspekte.de/die-juden-sind-nur-die-ersten-opfer-des-antisemitismus/; Accessed August 23, 2023.
399 See also https://jewishcurrents.org/the-strange-logic-of-germanys-antisemitism-bureaucrats. Accessed September 30, 2023.
400 See https://www.saarbruecker-zeitung.de/saarland/saarland-samuel-salzborn-im-interview-ueber-die-corona-proteste_aid-65884117; Accessed August 23, 2023. Or see https://www.bpb.de/shop/zeitschriften/apuz/verschwoerungstheorien-2021/339288/verschwoerungsmythen-und-antisemitismus/; Accessed August 23, 2023.
401 See https://www.saarbruecker-zeitung.de/saarland/saarland-samuel-salzborn-im-interview-ueber-die-corona-proteste_aid-65884117; Accessed August 23, 2023.

case of rare earths or coltan . . . With every step towards decarbonization, the promotion of renewable energies, education and the improvement of recycling, actors in politics, business and civil society cannot only promote environmental and climate protection, but also the rule of law, democracy, peace and overcoming antisemitic propaganda. Ideally, we can combine Baden-Württemberg's commitment with global responsibility and thus work for a world with less destruction, hatred, antisemitism, and racism.[402]

One could easily infer from this that a politicization of the institution is taking place.[403] Yet there is another way to view it, too. Once one already adheres to the most absurd claims of psychology and sees them as a tool, or even *the* tool, to understand and fight antisemitism, anything goes, so why not throwing Covid-19 and climate change into the mix, as well?

---

402 https://stm.baden-wuerttemberg.de/fileadmin/redaktion/dateien/PDF/190701_StM_Bericht_Beauftragter_gegen_Antisemitismus_B-W.pdf. Accessed August 23, 2023. The original text in German reads as follows: "Wenn wir den Antisemitismus global und glaubwürdig bekämpfen, für Demokratie und Rechtsstaatlichkeit einstehen wollen, dann muss dies auch stärkere Anstrengungen für die Wende zu erneuerbaren Energien und die Dekarbonisierung bedeuten. Die Verfeuerung fossiler Rohstoffe vergiftet nicht nur Umwelt und Klima, sondern verformt auch Gesellschaften, Staaten und religiöse Lehren ins Autoritäre. Gleichzeitig droht schon die Ausweitung neuer Abhängigkeiten etwa bei Seltenen Erden oder Coltan . . . Mit jedem Schritt zur Dekarbonisierung, der Förderung erneuerbarer Energien, von Bildung und der Verbesserung von Recycling können Akteure in Politik, Wirtschaft und Zivilgesellschaft nicht nur den Umwelt- und Klimaschutz fördern, sondern auch Rechtsstaatlichkeit, Demokratie, Frieden und die Überwindung antisemitischer Propaganda. Idealerweise können wir baden-württembergisches Engagement mit globaler Verantwortung verknüpfen und auch damit für eine Welt mit weniger Zerstörung, Hass, Antisemitismus und Rassismus wirken."

403 This is, unfortunately, an impression one gets of many of these commissioners. In August 2022, Mahmud Abbas had been invited to meet the German chancellor Olaf Scholz at his Kanzleramt in Berlin. At a press conference following the meeting, Abbas spoke – next to Scholz – of "50 holocausts" which Israel would commit. The fact that a German chancellor remained silent when this outrageous incident occurred (aside from the question of why Abbas was invited in the first place) led to much criticism. Hence, Felix Klein, the "Federal Commissioner for Jewish Life in Germany and the Fight Against Antisemitism," stepped in, defending Scholz in an interview. This was "above all a communication problem between the chancellor and his government spokesman," and "That pretty much says it all." As if a German chancellor wouldn't be able to switch a microphone on by himself at a press conference in his own office; and as if the commissioner's role is to silence critique of the government. See: https://www.tagesschau.de/inland/innenpolitik/klein-antisemitismusbeauftragter-101.html; Accessed August 23, 2023. Klein's official job description on the German Ministry of the Interior website also addresses his role in the promotion of research on antisemitism. I have asked him about this aspect of his duties, to which he responded to me via his assistant that this is "of course meant to be understood politically" (*selbstverständlich politisch zu verstehen*). It is not known to me whether Klein has spoken to anyone other than to me about this; See https://www.antisemitismusbeauftragter.de/Webs/BAS/DE/beauftragter/amt-und-person/amt-und-person-node.html. Accessed August 23, 2023.

Psychology's entering the political realm and the politicization of mental illness is a devilish game, as it undermines responsibility but can also be used to discredit justifiable political causes. An example comes from the U.S. Civil Rights Movement, in which black men were discredited as "schizophrenic." Jonathan M. Metzl documents this well in *The Protest Psychosis: How Schizophrenia Became a Black Disease*.[404] Labelling political or religious dissidents "insane" is a common practise in dictatorships, too. Numerous examples of the systematic political abuse of psychiatry in the Soviet Union speak to this.[405] It has, in fact, been estimated that about one-third of the political prisoners in the Soviet Union were imprisoned in psychiatric hospitals during the 1970s and 1980s.[406] When applied as a policy tool, psychology leads to unhelpful mix-ups and serves as a means to neglect human agency and judgement, of antisemites and heroes alike.

---

[404] Jonathan M. Metzl, *The Protest Psychosis: How Schizophrenia Became a Black Disease* (Boston: Beacon Press, 2010).
[405] See, for instance, the case of Vladimir Bukovskii: Philip Boobbyer, "Vladimir Bukovskii and Soviet Communism," *The Slavonic and East European Review* 87.3 (2009): 452–487.
[406] Robert van Voren, "Political Abuse of Psychiatry—An Historical Overview," *Schizophrenia Bulletin* 36.1 (2010): 33–35.

Conclusion

In life, it is not so much about staying mentally sane, but staying human that counts. And humans usually do not murder Jews, not even the insane ones. The fact that somebody is mentally ill does not explain antisemitism. Beliefs in antisemitic conspiracy myths can occur as part of paranoid states, schizophrenia and so on, but why do we so often find them in persons across many different socio-economic and cultural backgrounds, who are basically "sane and healthy," but hate the Jews? This book is a call for an end to triumphalist claims within psychology and its overemphasis on questions of sanity, while it urges the academic community to acknowledge that we simply don't know how the antisemitic mind works in psychological terms. As with other human problems, psychology does not so much explain but explains away the problem of antisemitism. But it needs to be prevented, or called out and judged, not therapized.

At the height of antisemitic violence in the United States in the summer of 2021, the American Psychological Association (APA) wrote on their website, under the headline "APA calls for end to continued antisemitic violence in US: Research shows hate crimes cause psychological damage to individuals and communities":

> APA's Resolution on Anti-Semitic and Anti-Jewish Prejudice calls on psychologists to act to eliminate all antisemitic discrimination. It commits APA to use its influence to promote fairness, respect and dignity for all people, regardless of religion or ethnicity, in all arenas in which psychologists work and practice, and in society at large . . . Psychological research shows that hate crimes create fear, anxiety and insecurity among victims and others in the community, leaving them feeling vulnerable, angry and depressed. These acts make people feel unsafe in their homes, their communities and their places of worship. Research demonstrates that acts of discrimination affect the immune systems of victims and those who witness hateful acts, and the effects of hate crimes change attitudes and behaviors at a societal level for years. Psychological science even shows that these vile acts cause long-lasting damage for perpetrators by desensitizing them to violence . . . There is much for us to do. We must bring together all that psychology has to offer to eradicate hate in all its forms.[407]

I understand this as a typical example of psychology as megalomania, delusion, and pseudo-science.[408] To take this apart: "Research shows hate crimes cause psychological damage to individuals and communities." I believe every reasonable person knows that crime causes damage, yet by inserting "psychological" into the headline, it suddenly sounds as if the field has just discovered a previously unknown fact. Nor did "psychological research" uncover that "hate crimes create

---

[407] https://www.apa.org/news/apa/2021/antisemitic-violence; Accessed August 23, 2023.
[408] I'm not aware of a clarification or further statement from the APA in this regard.

fear, and insecurity among victims and others in the community, leaving them feeling vulnerable, angry and depressed." The statement demonstrates how lightheartedly psychology takes ownership of common sense. Any reasonable person knows that "these acts make people feel unsafe in their homes, their communities and their places of worship," but by mentioning research on the "immune system" the whole statement receives a medical facade. And how does one solve the issue? By "eliminating all antisemitic discrimination." Yet, I am not aware of this having taken place; psychology has not to my knowledge successfully "eliminated" even a single case of antisemitism, let alone "all" of it. If only it were true that one could "bring together all that psychology has to offer to eradicate hate in all its forms." The successfully therapized antisemite remains wishful thinking at best. It almost seems as if the APA genuinely does not know the difference between science and daydreaming.[409]

The outbreak of antisemitic violence in the summer of 2021 was not a question of insanity, but of a misguided sense of morality. Most demonstrators were not insane but saw a deep moral cause in their hatred of Jews, which they viewed as a representation of Israel's side in the Middle East conflict. Populists on social media then enforced this "moral" cause, almost causing pogroms on American soil.[410] A misguided sense of morality is the question in these (potential) crimes against Jews, not insanity.

As it turns out, there is no clinical, or social, or forensic application of psychology that uncovers anything substantial about antisemitism. There is no therapy, no drug, no profiling technique or psychohistorical insights we could use either, even when we "bring together all that psychology has to offer." Instead, as Jew-hate appears on the right and the left and in between, the antisemitic mind remains something dangerous and unresolved in psychological terms. And even if psychology were to offer any meaningful insights, it cannot on its own produce any complete knowledge – as is so often claimed by psychologists – because the whole historical, sociological, cultural, religious, and economic context plays a role in the making of an antisemitic mind. In the words of Hegel, *Das Wahre ist das Ganze* ("The truth is the whole").[411]

To move forward we need to abandon pseudo-scientific ideas from court practice, the study of antisemitism, public policy, de-radicalization programs, and

---

[409] I came to this personal impression based on the evidence I have seen, and because I'm not aware of a clarification or further statement from the APA in this regard.
[410] In this context interesting: Stephen R. C. Hicks, *Nietzsche and the Nazis* (Roscoe, IL: Ockham's Razor Publishing, 2010).
[411] Georg W. F. Hegel, *Vorlesungen über die Philosophie der Religion* ("Lectures on the philosophy of religion") (Hamburg: Felix Meiner Verlag, 1993 (1821)).

the like. Yet, since psychology has created a whole climate of opinion in Western societies, this is an increasingly difficult thing to do. We also need to come up with a way to draw the line between disorders and mental health issues that genuinely impact the person's capability to make rational decisions, and those that do not. But who should draw the line? People who do not replace the practise of science with the mere appearance of it would be a good start.

Overall, psychology offers mostly dangerous ideas – as scientific discoveries can sometimes be. But it is tragic that most of psychology's ideas are not even based on proper science and scholarship, while they can set the stage for more Jew-hate. It should be clear that psychology's place in the prevention and judgement of antisemitic crimes is highly questionable. Most of its findings are not scientific in nature and should not be presented as such or, even worse, overrun the rule of law by facilitating the evasion of responsibility. Even Freud acknowledged in private the fact that "the case histories I write should read like short stories and that, as one might say, they lack the serious stamp of science,"[412] and further admitted the unscientific nature of his endeavour in a letter to his friend Wilhelm Fliess:

> I am actually not at all a man of science, not an observer, not an experimenter, not a thinker. I am by temperament nothing but a conquistador – an adventurer, if you want it translated – with all the curiosity, daring, and tenacity characteristic of a man of this sort. Such people are customarily esteemed only if they have been successful, have really discovered something; otherwise they are dropped by the wayside. And that is not altogether unjust.[413]

In the final analysis, the wayside it is. But more importantly, something can be of no value but still be perceived as a "discovery." And that makes psychology, especially regarding antisemitism, so dangerous, tragic, and altogether unjust.

---

[412] Quoted in Sheila Kohler, "Narrative Techniques in Freud's Case Histories," *The Yale Review* 103.1 (2015): 110.

[413] Letter 398 (1 February 1900) from the *Complete Letters of Sigmund Freud to Wilhelm Fliess*, quoted in Sarah Winter, *Freud and the Institution of Psychoanalytic Knowledge* (Stanford: Stanford University Press, 1999), 341n122.

Bibliography

Alexander, C. N. (1990). "Growth of Higher Stages of Consciousness: Maharishi's Vedic Psychology of Human Development." In C. N. Alexander and E. J. Langer (eds.), *Higher Stages of Human Development: Perspectives on Human Growth*, 286–341. New York: Oxford University Press.

Alison, L. J., M. D. Smith, O. Eastman, and L. Rainbow (2003). "Toulmin's philosophy of argument and its relevance to offender profiling," *Psychology, Crime, and Law* 9: 173–183.

Arendt, Hannah (1981). *The Life of the Mind: The Groundbreaking Investigation on How We Think*. New York: Harcourt.

Askay, Richard, and Jensen Farquhaar (2006). *Apprehending The Inaccessible: Freudian Psychoanalysis and Existential Phenomenology*. Evanston, IL: Northwestern University Press.

Bar-Tal, Daniel (2019). "The Challenges of Social and Political Psychology in Pursuit of Peace: Personal Account," *Peace and Conflict: Journal of Peace Psychology* 25.3: 182–197.

Bargh, J. A., M. Chen, and L. Burrows (1996). "Automaticity of social behavior: Direct effects of trait construct and stereotype activation on action," *Journal of Personality and Social Psychology* 71.2: 230–244

Baumeister, Roy F., and J. Tierney (2010). *Willpower: Why Self-Control is the Secret of Success*. London: Penguin.

Baumeister, Roy F. et al. (2003). "Does High Self-Esteem Cause Better Performance, Interpersonal Success, Happiness, or Healthier Lifestyles?" *Psychological Science in the Public Interest* 4.1: 1–44.

Beebe, John (2004). "Understanding consciousness through the theory of psychological types." In Joseph Cambray and Linda Carter (eds.), *Analytical Psychology: Contemporary Perspectives in Jungian Analysis*, 19–50. London: Routledge.

Berlinski, David (2009). *The Devil's Delusion: Atheism and Its Scientific*. 2nd Edition. New York: Basic Books.

Beller, Steven (2007). *Antisemitism: A Very Short Introduction*. Oxford: Oxford University Press.

Bem, D. J. (2011). "Feeling the future: Experimental evidence for anomalous retroactive influences on cognition and affect," *Journal of Personality and Social Psychology* 100: 407–425.

Boobbyer, Philip (2009). "Vladimir Bukovskii and Soviet Communism," *The Slavonic and East European Review* 87.3: 452–487.

Borum, R., R. Otto, and S. Golding (1993). "Improving clinical judgment and decision making in forensic evaluation," *The Journal of Psychiatry & Law* 21: 35–76.

Bourdieu, Pierre (2000). "The Biographical Illusion." In Paul du Gay, Jessica Evans, and Peter Redman (eds.), *Identity: A Reader*, 297–303. Los Angeles: Sage.

Boyd, R. (2017). *A Different Kind of Animal: How Culture Transformed Our Species*. Princeton: Princeton University Press.

Brannigan, Augustine (2017). *The Rise and Fall of Social Psychology: The Use and Misuse of the Experimental Method*. London: Routledge.

Brinkmann, Svend (2017). *Stand Firm: Resisting the Self-Improvement Craze*. New York: Polity.

Brunner, José (2008). "Eichmann's Mind: Psychological, Philosophical, and Legal Perspectives," *Tel Aviv University Law School Faculty Papers* 61: 23.

Burston, Daniel (2021). *Anti-Semitism and Analytical Psychology: Jung, Politics and Culture*. New York: Routledge.

Canter, David V., L. J. Alison, E. Alison, and N. Wentink (2004). "The organized/disorganized typology of serial murder: Myth or model?" *Psychology, Public Policy, and Law* 10: 293–320.

Cassuto, Leonard (2006). "The Silhouette and the Secret Self: Theorizing Biography in Our Times," *American Quarterly* 58: 1249–1261.

Chambers, Chris (2017). *The Seven Deadly Sins of Psychology: A Manifesto for Reforming the Culture of Scientific Practice*. Princeton: Princeton University Press.

Chomsky, Noam (1998). *Language and Problems of Knowledge: The Managua Lectures*. Cambridge, MA: MIT Press.

Claydon, L., and P. Catley (2021). "Thoughts on the Insanity Defence." In B. Brożek, J. Hage, and N. Vincent (eds.), *Law and Mind: A Survey of Law and the Cognitive Sciences*, 342–350. Cambridge: Cambridge University Press.

Clayton, Aubrey (2021). *Bernoulli's Fallacy: Statistical Illogic and the Crisis of Modern Science*. New York: Columbia University Press.

Cohen Abady, Florette (2020). "The Psychology of Modern Antisemitism: Theory, Research, and Methodology." In Armin Lange, Kerstin Mayerhofer, Dinat Porat, and Lawrence H. Schiffman (eds.), *Comprehending and Confronting Antisemitism: A Multifaceted Approach*, 271–296. Berlin: De Gruyter.

Coles, Robert (1975). *The Mind's Fate: Ways of Seeing Psychiatry and Psychoanalysis*. Boston: Little, Brown & Co.

Cousins, S. D. (1989). "Culture and self-perception in Japan and the United States," *Journal of Personality and Social Psychology* 56: 124–131.

Crews, Frederick (2017). *Freud: The Making of an Illusion*. New York: Metropolitan Books.

Cristea, I. A., C. Gentili, P. Pietrini, and P. Cuijpers (2017). "Sponsorship bias in the comparative efficacy of psychotherapy and pharmacotherapy for adult depression: meta-analysis," *British Journal of Psychiatry* 210.1: 16–23.

Croskerry, P. (2012). "Achieving Quality in Clinical Decision Making: Cognitive Strategies and Detection of Bias," *Academic Emergency Medicine Journal* 9: 1184–1204.

Cuddy, Amy J. C., Michael I. Norton, and Susan T. Fiske (2005). "This Old Stereotype: The Pervasiveness and Persistence of the Elderly Stereotype," *Journal of Social Issues* 61.2: 267–285.

Cuijpers, P., and I. A. Cristea (2015). "What if a placebo effect explained all the activity of depression treatments?" *World Psychiatry* 14.3: 310–311.

Cuijpers, P. et al. (2010). "The effects of psychotherapy for adult depression are overestimated: a meta-analysis of study quality and effect size," *Psychological Medicine* 40.2: 211–223.

Czech, H. (2018). "Hans Asperger, National Socialism, and "race hygiene" in Nazi-era Vienna," *Molecular Autism* 9.29.

Dalrymple, Theodore (2020). Admirable Evasions. Encounter Books.

Damrosch, Leo (2005). *Jean-Jacques Rousseau: Restless Genius*. New York: Houghton Mifflin.

Danziger, Shai, Jonathan Levav, and Liora Avnaim-Pesso (2011). "Extraneous Factors in Judicial Decisions," *Proceedings of the National Academy of Sciences of the United States of America* 108.17: 6889–6892.

Darwin, Charles (1871). *Descent of Man*. Appleton, NY: American Home Library Co.

Davis, Lennard J. (2010). "Obsession: Against Mental Health." In Jonathan M. Metzl and Anna Kirkland (eds.), *Against Health: How Health Became the New Morality*, 121–132. New York: New York University Press.

Dawes, Robyn M. (1996). *House of Cards: Psychology and Psychotherapy Built on Myth*. New York: The Free Press.

Downs, Donald Alexander (1996). *More Than Victims: Battered Women, the Syndrome Society, and the Law*. Chicago: The University of Chicago Press.

Doyen, S., O. Klein, C.-L. Pichon, and A. Cleeremans (2012). "Behavioral Priming: It's All in the Mind, but Whose Mind?" *PLoS ONE* 7.1: e29081.

Driessen, E. et al. (2015). "Does Publication Bias Inflate the Apparent Efficacy of Psychological Treatment for Major Depressive Disorder? A Systematic Review and Meta-Analysis of US National Institutes of Health-Funded Trials," *PLoS One* 10.9: e0137864.

Dutton, E. (2019). "Jewish Group Evolutionary Strategy Is the Most Plausible Hypothesis: a Response to Nathan Cofnas' Critical Analysis of Kevin MacDonald's Theory of Jewish Involvement in Twentieth Century Ideological Movements," *Evolutionary Psychological Science* 5: 136–142.

Earp, B. D., and D. Trafimow (2015). "Replication, falsification, and the crisis of confidence in social psychology," *Frontiers in Psychology* 6: 1–11.

Eisen, Robert (2021). *Judaism and Violence: A Historical Analysis with Insights from Social Psychology.* Cambridge: Cambridge University Press.

El-Mallakh, Rif S., Yonglin Gao, and R. Jeannie Roberts (2011). "Tardive dysphoria: The role of long term antidepressant use in-inducing chronic depression," *Medical Hypotheses* 76: 769–773.

Elliott, Carl (2010). "Pharmaceutical Propaganda." In Jonathan M. Metzl and Anna Kirkland (eds.), *Against Health: How Health Became the New Morality*, 93–104. New York: New York University Press.

Ellmann, Richard (1959). *James Joyce*. Oxford: Oxford University Press.

Epstein, William (2006). *Psychotherapy as Religion: The Civil Divine in America*. Reno: University of Nevada Press.

Epstein, William (1996). *The Illusion of Psychotherapy*. New York: Transaction Publishers.

Epstein, William (2013). *Empowerment as Ceremony*. New York: Transaction Publishers.

Epstein, William (2014). *Moral Psychology, Volume 4: Free Will and Moral Responsibility*. Cambridge, MA: MIT Press.

Erwin, E. (1997). *Psychotherapy and Philosophy*. New York: Sage.

Eysenck, Hans J. (1985). *Decline & Fall of the Freudian Empire*. London: Routledge.

Falk, Avner (2008). *Anti-Semitism: A History and Psychoanalysis of Contemporary Hatred*. Westport, CT: Praeger.

Faust, D. (2012). *Coping with psychiatric and psychological testimony*. 6th Edition. New York: Oxford University Press.

Fava, Giovanni A. (1995). "Holding On: Depression, Sensitization by Antidepressant Drugs, and Prodigal Experts," *Psychother Psychosom* 64: 57–61.

Feher, Shoshanah (1994). "Maintaining the Faith: The Jewish Anti-Cult and Counter-Missionary Movement." In Anson D. Shupe and David G. Bromley (eds.), *Anti-Cult Movements in Cross-Cultural Perspective*, 33–48. New York: Garland.

Feinberg, Joel (1970). *Doing and Deserving*. Princeton: Princeton University Press.

Feltham, C. (2013). *Counselling and Counselling Psychology: A Critical Examination*. Ross-on-Wye: PCCS Books.

Feltham, C. (2010). *"Whatever Happened to Free Will and Willpower?" Critical Thinking in Counselling and Psychotherapy*. London: Sage.

Fischer, John Martin, and Mark Ravizza, eds. (1993). *Perspectives on Moral Responsibility*. Ithaca, NY: Cornell University Press.

France, Peter, and William St. Clair, eds. (2000). *Mapping Lives: The Uses of Biography*. Oxford: Oxford University Press.

Francis, G. (2012). "The psychology of replication and replication in psychology," *Perspect. Psychol. Sci.* 7: 585–594.

Freud, Sigmund (1964). "Moses and Monotheism: three essays." In James Strachey (ed.), *The standard edition of the complete psychological works of Sigmund Freud, Volume XXIII (1937–1939): Moses and Monotheism, an outline of psycho-analysis and other works*, 87–92. London: Hogarth Press.
Friedländer, Saul (2013). *Franz Kafka: The Poet of Shame and Guilt*. New Haven: Yale University Press.
Frosh, Stephen (2008). "Freud and Jewish Identity," *Theory and Psychology* 18.2: 167–178.
Frosh, Stephen (2006). *For And Against Psychoanalysis*. 2nd Edition. New York: Routledge.
Frosh, Stephen (2005). *Hate and the "Jewish Science": Anti-Semitism, Nazism and Psychoanalysis*. New York: Palgrave Macmillan.
Frosh, Stephen (2004). "Freud, Psychoanalysis and Anti-Semitism," *The Psychoanalytic Review* 91: 309–330.
Furedi, Frank (2016). "The Cultural Underpinning of Concept Creep," *Psychological Inquiry* 27:1, 34–39.
Garrison, Katie E., David Tang, and Brandon J. Schmeichel (2016). "Embodying Power," *Social Psychological and Personality Science* 7.7: 623–630.
Gelfand, M. (2019). *Rule Makers, Rule Breakers: Tight and Loose Cultures and the Secret Signals that Direct our Lives*. New York: Scribner.
Geller, Jay Howard (2019). *The Scholems: A Story of the German-Jewish Bourgeoisie from Emancipation to Destruction*. Ithaca, NY: Cornell University Press.
Goodman, David G. (2011). "The Protocols of the Elders of Zion in Japan." In Esther Webman (ed.), *The Global Impact of The Protocols of the Elders of Zion: A Century-old Myth*, 161–174. New York: Routledge.
Grove, W. M., D. H. Zald, B. S. Lebow, B. E. Snitz, and C. Nelson (2000). "Clinical vs. mechanical prediction: A meta-analysis," *Psychological Assessment* 12: 19–30.
Hage, Jaap, and Antonia Waltermann (2021). "Responsibility, Liability, and Retribution." In B. Brożek, J. Hage, and N. Vincent (eds.), *Law and Mind: A Survey of Law and the Cognitive Sciences*, 255–288. Cambridge: Cambridge University Press.
Hall, Edward T. (1976). *Beyond Culture*. New York: Anchor Books.
Harrington, Anne (2019). *Mind Fixers: Psychiatry's Troubled Search for the Biology of Mental Illness*. New York: W.W. Norton & Co.
Haslam, Nick (2016). "Concept Creep: Psychology's Expanding Concepts of Harm and Pathology," *Psychological Inquiry* 27:1, 1–17.
Hart, H. L. A. (1968). *Punishment and Responsibility. Essays in the Philosophy of Law*. Oxford: Clarendon.
Haybron, D. M. (2008). *The Pursuit of Unhappiness: The Elusive Psychology of Well-Being*. Oxford: Oxford University Press.
Healy, D. (2012). *Pharmageddon*. Berkeley: University of California Press.
Healy, D. (2004). "Shaping Discontent: The Roles of Science and Marketing." In P. Pietikainen (ed.), *Modernity and Its Discontents: Sceptical Essays on the Psychomedical Management of Malaise*. Stockholm: Axel and Margaret Johnson Foundation.
Hegel, George W. F. (1993 (1821)). *Vorlesungen über die Philosophie der Religion*. Hamburg: Felix Meiner Verlag.
Helson, Ravenna, Virginia S.Y Kwan, Oliver P. John, and Constance Jones (2002). "The growing evidence for personality change in adulthood: Findings from research with personality inventories," *Journal of Research in Personality* 36.4: 287–306.
Hengartner, Michael P. (2018). "Raising Awareness for the Replication Crisis in Clinical Psychology by Focusing on Inconsistencies in Psychotherapy Research: How Much Can We Rely on Published Findings from Efficacy Trials?" *Frontiers in psychology* 9: 1–5.

Henrich, Joseph (2020). *The WEIRDest People in the World: How the West Became Psychologically Peculiar and Particularly Prosperous*. New York: Farrar, Straus & Giroux.

Henrich, J., S. J. Heine, and A. Norenzayan (2010). "The weirdest people in the world?" *Behavioral and Brain Sciences* 33.2–3: 61–83.

Herf, Jeffrey. Review of *Nazis und der Nahe Osten: Wie der Islamische Antisemitismus Entstand*, by Matthias Küntzel. *Antisemitism Studies* 5, no. 1 (2021): 218–229.

Hicks, Stephen R. C. (2010). *Nietzsche and the Nazis*. Roscoe, IL: Ockham's Razor Publishing.

Hilton, N. Z., G. T. Harris, and M. E. Rice (2006). "Sixty-six years of research on the clinical versus actuarial prediction of violence," *The Counseling Psychologist* 34: 400–409.

Homant, R. J., and D. B. Kennedy (1998). "Psychological aspects of crime scene profiling," *Criminal Justice and Behavior* 25: 319–343.

Horgan, John. (2000). *The Undiscovered Mind: How the Brain Defies Explanation*. London: Phoenix.

Horvilleur, Delphine (2021). *Anti-Semitism Revisited*. London: MacLehose Press.

Hume, David (2006 (1776)). *Enquiry Concerning Human Understanding: A Critical Edition*. Oxford: Oxford University Press.

Ioannidis, P. A. (2020). "Correction: Why Most Published Research Findings Are False," *PLoS Medicine* 19.8: e1004085.

Jackson, Craig, David Wilson, and Baljit Kaur Rana (2011). "The usefulness of criminal profiling," *Criminal Justice Matters* 84.1: 6–7.

Jaspal, Rusi (2023). "The social psychology of contemporary antisemitism," *Israel Affairs* 29: 31–51.

Jaspal, Rusi (2016). *Antisemitism and Anti-Zionism: Representation, Cognition and Everyday Talk*. London: Routledge.

Johansson, Magnus, and Elisabeth Punzi (2019). "Jewishness and psychoanalysis – the relationship to identity, trauma and exile. An interview study," *Jewish Culture and History* 20.2: 140–152.

Jones, E. (1951). "The psychology of the Jewish question." In *Essays in applied psychoanalysis, Vol. 1*. London: Hogarth.

Jung, Carl J. (1970). "Civilization in Transition." In Gerhard Adler, Michael Fordham, and Sir Herbert Read (eds.), *Collected Works of C. G. Jung: Volume 10*, 157–173. 2nd Edition. Translated by R. F. C. Hull. Princeton: Princeton University Press.

Kafka, Franz (2015). *Letters to Milena*. Translated by Philip Boehm. New York: Schocken.

Kagan, Jerome et. Al (1978). *Infancy: Its Place in Human Development*. Cambridge, MA: Harvard University Press.

Kahneman, Daniel (2012). *Thinking, Fast and Slow*. New York: Penguin.

Kain, Richard M. (1974). "An Interview with Carola Giedion-Weckler and Maria Jolas," *James Joyce Quarterly* 11.2: 94–122.

Kates, Allen R. (1999). *CopShock, Surviving Posttraumatic Stress Disorder (PTSD)*. Cortaro, AZ: Holbrook Street Press.

Kenneth, Jeannette (2001). *Agency and Responsibility*. Oxford: Clarendon.

Khan, A., J. Faucett, P. Lichtenberg, I. Kirsch, W. A. Brown (2012). "A systematic review of comparative efficacy of treatments and controls for depression," *PLoS One* 7.7: e41778.

Kirkpatrick, Lee A., and Carlos David Navarrete (2006). "Reports of My Death Anxiety Have Been Greatly Exaggerated: A Critique of Terror Management Theory from an Evolutionary Perspective," *Psychological Inquiry* 17.4: 288–298.

Kirsch, Irving (2011). *The Emperor's New Drugs: Exploding the Antidepressant Myth*, New York: Basic Books.

Kirsch, Thomas (2000). *The Jungians: A Comparative and Historical Perspective*. New York: Routledge.

Klafter, Andrew (Nachum) (2020). "Anti-Semitism: A Psychoanalytic Perspective." In H. Steven Moffic et al. (eds.), *Anti-Semitism and Psychiatry: Recognition, Prevention, and Interventions*, 163–181. New York: Springer.

Kocsis, R. N., A. F. Hayes, and H. J. Irwin (2002). "Investigative experience and accuracy in psychological profiling of a violent crime," *Journal of Interpersonal Violence* 17: 811–823.

Kohler, Sheila (2015). "Narrative Techniques in Freud's Case Histories," *The Yale Review* 103.1: 110.

Kuhn, M. H., and T. S. McPartland (1954). "An empirical investigation of self-attitude," *American Sociological Review* 19: 68–76.

Lange, Armin, Kerstin Mayerhofer, Dinat Porat, and Lawrence H. Schiffman, eds. (2019). *Comprehending and Confronting Antisemitism*. Berlin: De Gruyter.

Langer, Walter C. (1972). *The Mind of Adolf Hitler: The Secret Wartime Report*. New York: Basic Books.

Larrick, R. P. (2004). "Debiasing." In D. J. Koehler and N. Harvey (eds.), *Blackwell Handbook of Judgment and Decision Making*, 316–337. Malden, MA: Blackwell.

Leichsenring, F. et al., (2017). "Biases in research: risk factors for non-replicability in psychotherapy and pharmacotherapy research," *Psychological Medicine* 47.6: 1000–1011.

Leland, P. (2018). "Unconscious Representations in Kant's Early Writings," *Kantian Review* 23.2: 257–284.

Lifton, R. J. (1989). *The Nazi doctors: Medical killing and the psychology of genocide*. London: Little, Brown & Co.

Lihong, Song (2016). "Reflections on Chinese Jewish Studies: A Comparative Perspective." In James Ross and Song Lihong (eds.), *The Image of Jews in Contemporary China*, 206–234. Brookline, MA: Academic Studies Press.

Lilienfeld, Scott O., Steven Jay Lynn, John Ruscio, and Barry L. Beyerstein (2009). *50 Great Myths of Popular Psychology: Shattering Widespread Misconceptions about Human Behavior*. Malden, MA: Wiley-Blackwell.

Loewenthal, Kate Miriam, and Barry Marcus (2020). "Jewish Stereotypes in Psychiatric Diagnosis and Treatment." In H. Steven Moffic et al. (eds.), *Anti-Semitism and Psychiatry: Recognition, Prevention, and Interventions*, 185–192. New York: Springer.

Loftus, Elizabeth (1994). *The Myth of Repressed Memory: False Memories and Allegations of Sexual Abuse*. New York: St. Martin's Griffin.

Loftus, Elizabeth F., and Jacqueline E. Pickell (1995). "The Formation of False Memories," *Psychiatric Annals* 25.12: 720–725.

Luborsky, L. et al. (1999). "The researcher's own therapy allegiances: a "wild card" in comparisons of treatment efficacy," *Clin. Psychol. Sci. Pract.* 6: 95–106.

Lucy, William (2007). *Philosophy of Private Law*. Oxford: Oxford University Press.

MacDonald, Kevin (1998). *The Culture of Critique: An Evolutionary Analysis of Jewish Involvement in Twentieth-Century Intellectual and Political Movements*. Westport, CT: Praeger.

MacDonald, Kevin (1994). *A People That Shall Dwell Alone: Judaism as a Group Evolutionary Strategy*. Westport, CT: Praeger.

Mackay, R. D. (1995). *Mental Condition Defences in the Criminal Law*. Oxford: Clarendon.

Malleson, Andrew (2005). *Whiplash and Other Useful Illnesses*. Montreal: McGill-Queen's University Press.

Mandelbrot, Benoit (1967). "How Long Is the Coast of Britain? Statistical Self-Similarity and Fractal Dimensions," *Science* 156: 636–638.

Marcus, Kenneth L. (2015). *The Definition of Anti-Semitism*. Oxford: Oxford University Press.

Marcus, Kenneth L. (2012). "Accusation in a Mirror," *Loyola University Chicago Law Journal* 43: 357–393.

Masson, Jeffrey Moussaieff (1988). *Against Therapy: Emotional Tyranny and the Myth of Psychological Healing*. New York: Athenaeum.
McCrae, R. R., A. Terracciano, and 79 Members of the Personality Profiles of Cultures Project (2005). "Personality profiles of cultures: Aggregate personality traits," *Journal of Personality and Social Psychology* 89: 407–425.
McDonald, Peter (2004). *The Oxford Dictionary of Medical Quotations*. Oxford: Oxford University Press.
McGuire, William, and R. F. C. Hull, eds. (1977). *C.G. Jung Speaking: Interviews and Encounters*. Princeton: Princeton University Press.
Meehl, P. E. (1956). "Wanted: A good cookbook," *American Psychologist* 11: 263–272.
Melamed, Huval (2010). "Mentally Ill Persons Who Commit Crimes: Punishment or Treatment?" *Journal of the American Academy of Psychiatry and the Law* 38.1: 100–103.
Metzl, Jonathan M., and Anna Kirkland, eds. (2010). *Against Health: How Health Became the New Morality*. New York: New York University Press.
Metzl, Jonathan M. (2010). *The Protest Psychosis: How Schizophrenia Became a Black Disease*. Boston: Beacon Press.
Metzl, Jonathan M. (2003). *Prozac on the Couch: Prescribing Gender in the Era of Wonder Drugs*. Durham, NC: Duke University Press.
Meynen, Gerben (2021). "The Insanity Defense." In B. Brożek, J. Hage, and N. Vincent (eds.), *Law and Mind: A Survey of Law and the Cognitive Sciences*, 331–332. Cambridge: Cambridge University Press.
Moffic, H. Steven (2020). "Is There a Cure for Anti-Semitism?" In H. Steven Moffic et al. (eds.), *Anti-Semitism and Psychiatry: Recognition, Prevention, and Interventions*, 343–359. New York: Springer.
Moffic, H. Steven et al., eds. (2020). *Anti-Semitism and Psychiatry: Recognition, Prevention, and Interventions*. New York: Springer.
Moloney, Paul (2013). *The Therapy Industry: The Irresistible Rise of the Talking Cure, and Why It Doesn't Work*. London: Pluto Press.
Moncrieff, J., R. E. Cooper, T. Stockmann et al. (2022). "The serotonin theory of depression: a systematic umbrella review of the evidence," Mol Psychiatry.
Moody, A. David (2015). *Ezra Pound: Poet. A Portrait of the Man and His Work. III: The Tragic Years 1939–1972*. Oxford: Oxford University Press.
Moratti, S., and D. Patterson, eds. (2016). *Legal Insanity and the Brain: Science, Law and European Courts*. Oxford: Hart.
Morpurco, V. E. (2007). "Why does Moses and Monotheism still make us uneasy? Freud, psychoanalysis anti-Semitism," *The Italian Psychoanal Annual* 1: 203–220.
Morrock, Richard (2012). "'The Ancient Enemy': The Psychology of Anti-Semitism The Journal of Psychohistory," *New York* 40.2: 103–114.
Moskowitz, Eva S. (2001). *In Therapy We Trust: America's Obsession with Self-Fulfillment*. Baltimore: The Johns Hopkins University Press.
Moyer, M. (2019). "People drawn to conspiracy theories share a cluster of psychological features," *SciAm* 320.3: 58–63.
Munro, Donald (1985). "Introduction." In *Individualism and Holism: Studies in Confucian and Taoist Values*, 1–34. Ann Arbor: University of Michigan Press.
Muthukrishna, M., A. H. Bell, J. Henrich et al. (2020). "Beyond Western, Educated, Industrial, Rich, and Democratic (WEIRD) Psychology: Measuring and Mapping Scales of Cultural and Psychological Distance," *Psychological Science* 31.6: 678–701.
Nabokov, Vladimir (1990). "Interview with Alvin Toffler." In *Strong Opinions*, 17–38. London: Penguin.

Navarrete, Carlos David, and Daniel M. T. Fessel (2005). "Normative Bias and Adaptive Challenges: A Relational Approach to Coalitional Psychology and a Critique of Terror Management Theory," *Evolutionary Psychology* 3.1: 297–325.

Newman, Leonard S., and Ralph Erber, eds. (2002). *Understanding Genocide: The Social Psychology of the Holocaust*. Oxford: Oxford University Press.

Newnes, Craig (2021). "Judaism and the psy project." In Craig Newnes (ed.), *Racism in Psychology: Challenging Theory, Practice and Institutions*. New York: Routledge.

Nickerson, R. S. (2004). *Cognition and chance: The psychology of probabilistic reasoning*. Mahwah, NJ: Lawrence Erlbaum Associates.

Ostow, Mortimer (1996). *Myth and Madness. The Psychodynamics of Antisemitism*. New York: Transaction Publishers.

Packer, Sharon (2020). "How Anti-Semitism and the Shoah Helped Shape Twentieth-Century Psychiatry." In H. Steven Moffic et al. (eds.), *Anti-Semitism and Psychiatry: Recognition, Prevention, and Interventions*, 83–97. New York: Springer.

Parker, Ian (2014 (1989)). *The Crisis in Modern Social Psychology and How to End It*. London: Routledge.

Pawel, Ernst (2011). *The Labyrinth of Exile: A Life of Theodor Herzl*. New York: Farrar, Straus & Giroux.

Penslar, Derek (2020). *Theodor Herzl: The Charismatic Leader*. New Haven: Yale University Press.

Penslar, Derek (2019). "Zionism as Theodor Herzl's Life Project." In Nina Caputo and Mitchell B. Hart, (eds.), *On the Word of a Jew: Religion, Reliability, and the Dynamics of Trust*, 276–296. Bloomington: Indiana University Press.

Perry, Gina (2012). *Behind the Shock Machine: the untold story of the notorious Milgram psychology experiments*. New York: The New Press.

Perry, Gina, et al. (2019). "Credibility and Incredulity in Milgram's Obedience Experiments: A Reanalysis of an Unpublished Test," *Social Psychology Quarterly* 83.1: 88–106.

Pigott, H. E., A. M. Leventhal, G. S. Alter, and J. J. Boren (2010). "Efficacy and Effectiveness of Antidepressants: Current Status of Research," *Psychother Psychosom* 79: 267–279.

Popper, Karl (1963). *Conjectures and Refutations: The Growth of Scientific Knowledge*. London: Routledge.

Popper, Karl (1959). *The Logic of Scientific Discovery*. London: Routledge.

Posternak, Michael A. et al. (2006). "The Naturalist Course of Unipolar Major Depression in the Absence of Somatic Therapy," *The Journal of Nervous and Mental Disease* 194.5: 324–329.

Pytell, T. E. (2003). "Redeeming the unredeemable: Auschwitz and man's search for meaning," *Holocaust and Genocide Studies* 17.1: 89–113.

Rad, M. S., A. J. Martingano, and J. Ginges (2018). "Toward a psychology of Homo sapiens: Making psychological science more representative of the human population," *Proceedings of the National Academy of Sciences* 115: 11401–11405.

Radics, George Baylon, and Vineeta Sinha (2018). "Regulation of Religion and Granting of Public Holidays: The Case of Tai Pucam in Singapore," *Asian Journal of Social Science* 46.4–5: 524–548.

Radics, George Baylon, and Poon Yee Suan (2016). "Amos Yee, Free Speech, and Maintaining Religious Harmony in Singapore," *University of Pennsylvania Asian Law Review* 12.2.

Ranehill, E., A. Dreber, M. Johannesson, S. Leiberg, S. Sul, and R. A. Weber (2015). "Assessing the Robustness of Power Posing: No Effect on Hormones and Risk Tolerance in a Large Sample of Men and Women," *Psychological Science* 26.5: 653–656.

Rilke, Rainer Maria (2006). "Letter to Lou Andreas-Salomé, 20. Jan. 1912." In *Rainer Maria Rilke and Lou Andreas-Salomé: The Correspondence*, ed. and translated by Edward Snow and Michael Winkler, New York: Norton.

Ritchie, Stuart. (2020). *Science Fictions: Exposing Fraud, Bias, Negligence, and Hype in Science*. New York: Vintage.
Rodríguez-Ferreiro, J., I. Barberia, J. González-Guerra, and M. A. Vadillo (2019). "Are we truly special and unique? A replication of Goldenberg et al. (2001)," *R Soc Open Sci.* 6: 191114.
Rosenhan, D. L. (1973). "On Being Sane in Insane Places," *Science* 179: 250–258.
Rosenman, Stanley (1998). "A critique of classical psychoanalytic theories of anti-Semitism: a commentary on M. Ostrow's myth and madness: the psychodynamics of anti-Semitism," *The American Journal of Psychoanalysis* 58.4: 417–433.
Ruben, Theodore Isaac (1990). *Anti-Semitism: A Disease of the Mind – A Psychiatrist Explores the Psychodynamics of a Symbol Sickness*. New York: Continuum.
Sabel, Robbie (2016). "A Role for International Law in Combating Antisemitism?" *Israel Journal of Foreign Affairs* 10.3: 451–456.
Salaw-Hanslmaier, Stefanie (2003). *Die Rechtsnatur der Deutschen Forschungsgemeinschaft: Auswirkungen auf den Rechtsschutz des Antragstellers*. Hamburg: Verlag Dr. Kovač.
Salero, Steve (2005). *Sham: How the Self-Help Movement Made America Helpless*. New York: Crown Forum.
Salzborn, Samuel (2010). "Zur Politischen Psychologie des Antisemitismus," *Journal für Psychologie* 18.1: 1–22.
Sartre, Jean-Paul (1976 (1948)). *Anti-Semite and Jew: An Exploration of the Etiology of Hate*. New York: Schocken.
Scarry, Elaine (1985). *The Body in Pain: The Making and Unmaking of the World*. New York: Oxford University Press.
Schacter, Daniel L., Daniel Wegner, and Daniel Gilbert (2007). *Psychology*. New York: Worth.
Schilling, Christopher L. (2023). *The Japanese Talmud: Antisemitism in East Asia*. London: Hurst.
Schilling, Christopher L. (2023). "Why East Asia Matters to the Understanding of Antisemitism," *Journal of Contemporary Antisemitism* 6.2 (Fall Issue 2023).
Schilling, Christopher L. (2021). *Zen Judaism: The Case Against a Contemporary American Phenomenon*. New York: Palgrave Macmillan.
Schilling, Christopher L. (2021). "Buddhist Anti-Semitism," *Jewish Political Studies Review* 31.3-4 (22 February).
Schilling, Christopher L. (2020). "On Symbolic Philosemitism in Japan," *Journal of Modern Jewish Studies* 19.3: 297–313.
Schilling, Christopher L. (2020). "The Strange Absence of LGBTQ Actors in the Historical and Political Writings of Derek J. Penslar," *Harvard Kennedy School LGBTQ Policy Journal* 1.
Schilling, Christopher L. (2019). "Japanese Studies in Israel – A Response to Meron Medzini's 'From Alienation to Partnership: Israel-Japan Relation' in the Contemporary Review of the Middle East," *Japan Studies Review* XXIII.
Schilling, Christopher L. (2018). "Jewish Seoul: An Analysis of Philo- and Antisemitism in South Korea," *Modern Judaism: A Journal of Jewish Ideas and Experience* 38.2.
Schilling, Christopher L. (2018). "The Problem of Romanticizing Israel-Taiwan Relations," *Israel Affairs* 24.3: 460–466.
Schoenfeld, C. G. (1966). "Psychoanalysis and anti-Semitism," *Psychoanalytic Review* 53.1: 24–37.
Schopenhauer, Arthur (1886). *The World as Will and Idea*. London: Ludgate Hill.
Seymour, David (2007). *Law, Antisemitism and the Holocaust*. London: Routledge.
Sheffer, Edith (2018). *Asperger's Children: The Origins of Autism in Nazi Vienna*. New York: W.W. Norton & Co.

Sher, D. A., and J. L. Gibson (2021). "Pioneering, prodigious and perspicacious: Grunya Efimovna Sukhareva's life and contribution to conceptualising autism and schizophrenia," *Eur Child Adolesc Psychiatry* 32.3: 475–490.

Sigal, Jesse (2021). *The Quick Fix: Why Fad Psychology Can't Cure Our Social Ills*. New York: Farrar, Straus & Giroux.

Simmons, J. P., L. D. Nelson, and U. Simonsohn (2011). "False-positive psychology: undisclosed flexibility in data collection and analysis allows presenting anything as significant," *Psychol. Sci.* 22: 1359–1366.

Sinnott-Armstrong, Walter, ed. (2014). *Moral Psychology, Volume 4: Free Will and Moral Responsibility*. Cambridge, MA: MIT Press.

Sinnott-Armstrong, Walter, and Lynn Nadel, eds. (2011). *Conscious Will and Responsibility*. Oxford: Oxford University Press.

Sladeczek, I. E., F. Dumont, C. A. Martel, and A. Karagiannakis (2006). "Making sense of client data: Clinical experience and confirmation revisited," *American Journal of Psychotherapy* 60: 375–391.

Slobogin, Christopher (2018). "Introduction to this Special Issue: The Characteristics of Insanity and the Insanity Evaluation Process," *Behavioral Sciences and the Law* 36.3: 271–275.

Snook, Brent, R. M. Cullen, C. Bennell, P. J. Taylor, and P. Gendreau (2008). "The Criminal Profiling Illusion: What's Behind the Smoke and Mirrors?" *Criminal Justice and Behavior* 35.10: 1257–1276.

St. Clair, William (2000). "The Biographer as Archaeologist." In Peter France and William St. Clair (eds.), *Mapping Lives: The Uses of Biography*, 219–234. Oxford: Oxford University Press, 2000.

Stannard, David (1980). *Shrinking History: On Freud and the Failure of Psychohistory*. Oxford: Oxford University Press.

Staub, Ervin (1989). *The Roots of Evil: The Origins of Genocide and Other Group Violence*. New York: Cambridge University Press.

Steinberg, Gerald M.. "The Central Political Role of German Left Actors in the Campaign to Replace the IHRA Working Definition of Antisemitism", *Journal of Contemporary Antisemitism* 5, no. 2 (2022): 67–82.

Stoloff, Jean-Claude (2020). "Understanding the Current Resurgence of Anti-Semitism: The Situation in France." In H. Steven Moffic et al. (eds.), *Anti-Semitism and Psychiatry: Recognition, Prevention, and Interventions*, 267–278. New York: Springer.

Szasz, Thomas (1990). *Anti-Freud: Karl Kraus's Criticism of Psycho-analysis and Psychiatry*. Syracuse: Syracuse University Press.

Székely, Lajos (1988). "Tradition and infantile fantasy in the shape of modern antisemitism," *Scandinavian Psychoanalytical Review*, 11.2: 160–177.

Taylor, Shelley (1989). *Positive Illusions: Creative Self-Deception and the Healthy Mind*. New York: Basic Books.

Thornton, E. M. (1986). *The Freudian Fallacy: Freud and Cocaine*. London: Grafton Books.

Tolstoy, Leo (2004). *Anna Karenina*. New York: Penguin.

Tolstoy, Leo (2012). *The Devil and other Short Stories*. Translated by Louise and Aylmer Maude. Oxford: Oxford University Press.

Totton, Nick (1999). "'The baby and the bathwater': 'professionalisation' in psychotherapy and counselling," *British Journal of Guidance and Counselling* 27.3: 313–324.

Trilling, Lionel (1955). *Freud and the Crisis of Our Culture*. Boston: Beacon Press.

van Voren, Robert (2010). "Political Abuse of Psychiatry – An Historical Overview," *Schizophrenia Bulletin* 36.1: 33–35.

Vincent, Nicole A., ed. (2013). *Neuroscience and Legal Responsibility*. Oxford: Oxford University Press.

Waite, R. G. L. (1971). "Adolf Hitler's guilt feeling: a problem in history and psychology," *Journal of Interdisciplinary History* 1.2: 229–249.
Waller, James (2007). *Becoming Evil: How Ordinary People Commit Genocide and Mass Killing*. Oxford: Oxford University Press.
Watters, Ethan (2010). *Crazy Like Us: The Globalization of the American Psyche*. New York: The Free Press.
Watts, T. W., G. J. Duncan, and H. Quan (2018). "Revisiting the Marshmallow Test: A Conceptual Replication Investigating Links Between Early Delay of Gratification and Later Outcomes," *Psychological Science* 29.7: 1159–1177
Webster, Richard (2005). *Why Freud Was Wrong: Sin, Science and Psychoanalysis*. New York: Basic Books.
Weitzman, Steven (2017). *The Origins of the Jews: The Quest for Roots in a Rootless Age*. Princeton: Princeton University Press.
Wertham, Fredric (1968). *A Sign for Cain: An Exploration of Human Violence*. London: Robert Hale.
White, Alan R. (1985). *Grounds of Liability: An Introduction to the Philosophy of Law*. Oxford: Clarendon.
White, M. D., ed. (2017). *The Insanity Defense: Multidisciplinary Views on Its History, Trends and Controversies*. Santa Barbara: Praeger.
Whyte, L. L. (1978). *The Unconscious Before Freud*. New York: St. Martin's Press.
Williams, R. (1983). "Freudian psychology." In A. Richardson and J. Bowden (eds.), *A New Dictionary of Christian Theology*. London: SCM Press.
Wilson, D., C. A. Jackson, and B. Rana (2010). "Against the medical- psychological tradition of understanding serial killing by studying the killers: The case of BTK," *Amicus Journal* 22: 8–16.
Winter, Sarah (1999). *Freud and the Institution of Psychoanalytic Knowledge*. Stanford: Stanford University Press.
Wisse, Ruth (1994). "Holocaust, or War Against the Jews?" In Michael Brown (ed.), *Approaches to Antisemitism: Context and Curriculum*, 24–31. New York: The American Jewish Committee.
Wistrich, Robert S. (1992). *Antisemitism: The Longest Hatred*. New York: Pantheon.
Witkowski, Tomasz, and Maciej Zatonski (2015). *Psychology Gone Wrong: The Dark Sides of Science and Therapy*. Boca Raton, FL: Brown Walker Press.
Witkowski, Tomasz (2016). *Psychology Led Astray: Cargo Cult in Science and Therapy*. Boca Raton, FL: Brown Walker Press.
Witkowski, Tomasz (2020). *Shaping Psychology: Perspectives on Legacy, Controversy and the Future of the Field*. New York: Palgrave Macmillan.
Yerushalmi, Yosef Hayim (2011 (1982)). *Zakhor: Jewish History and Jewish Memory*. Seattle: University of Washington Press.

www.ingramcontent.com/pod-product-compliance
Lightning Source LLC
Chambersburg PA
CBHW031835230426
43669CB00009B/1364